710.

D1231659

HOWL OF THE CENSOR

HOWL
OF THE CENSOR

Edited with introduction by J. W. Ehrlich

Nourse Publishing Company

Box 398   San Carlos, California

KF
224
.F4
E45

*The poem HOWL FOR CARL SOLOMON copyright 1956,
by Allen Ginsberg; published by City Lights Books.
The introduction copyright 1961, by J. W. Ehrlich.
All rights reserved. No part of this book may
be reproduced without the permission of the
publisher, except by a reviewer who may quote
brief passages to be printed in a magazine or
newspaper.
Manufactured in the United States of America
by the H. Wolff Book Manufacturing Co.*
FIRST EDITION

s2.

145643

'Tis not the wholesome sharp morality,
Or modest anger of a satiric spirit,
That hurts or wounds the body of a state,
But the sinister application
Of the malicious, ignorant, and base
Interpreter; who will distort and strain
The general scope and purpose of an author
To his particular and private spleen.

BEN JONSON

INTRODUCTION

This is the history of a trial. In the Howl Of The Censor I have given the actual court proceedings, after some editing of the testimony and the arguments on the law. But first, some information about censorship and its origins as well as some of its history through the years.

In ancient Rome, appointed censors were arbiters of the political and social position of every freeman. Judicial functions, and the control of morals, fashion and speech, which we associate with censorship flowed naturally from that part of the functions of the two Roman censors which had to do with their establishment of standards of conduct for Roman citizens.

The modern theory of censorship assumes that established institutions of authority and the beliefs and customs which support them are essentially good. Individual liberty of self-expression must not be allowed to jeopardize the existing mores of the community.

Authoritarians believe that men are innately weak, full of sin, and prone to error. The masses must therefore be guided, controlled and restrained in their ideas and behavior and forced to respect the established morality, property rights, and constituted authority.

Libertarians agree that the state has the right to control behavior in the interests of the national group, but believe free discussion to be of inestimable value to the community. That with such freedom there is little danger of special interest groups using the power of legal authority to suppress freedom of expression. Liberals, in general, oppose censorship.

When the church ruled, heresy was warred against. With the advent of Victorian morality, sex became the target. According to Tacitus, Emperor Augustus was the first ruler who undertook to punish spoken or written words. He ordered the works of Labienus, who criticized the Government, to be burned. The historian Corus, who was too outspoken to please Tiberius, was left to starve to death, and his books were burned. Thinking himself libeled, Emperor Domitian ordered that Hermogenes, and all those who had circulated his writings, be crucified.

The English Crown forbade all printing except by royal license. Presses were maintained under close governmental supervision, and were subject to the decrees of the Star Chamber. In 1557 the Stationer's Company of London received the exclusive privilege of printing and publishing in the English dominions. In 1586, each university was allowed one printing press. Queen Elizabeth demanded that all books be read and passed by loyal bishops and councillors before publication. In the same year, the Star Chamber decreed that all works be examined in manuscript and licensed by the Archbishop of Canterbury. Penalties, such as the cropping of ears, the branding of foreheads, and the slitting of noses, were prescribed for violators. Precensorship of the press continued until it was abolished in 1695.

In 1637 Thomas Morton of the Plymouth Plantation wrote a book called The New English Canaan, printed in Amsterdam, in which he attacked the conduct of the authorities at the plantation. He was imprisoned for a year. Subsequently Philip Ratcliff was convicted "of most foul scandalous invective against our churches and government, was sentenced to be whipped, lose his ears, and be banished from the plantation, which was presently executed."

Political and religious control of books preceded sex censorship by hundreds of years. The English common law was slow to recognize the crime of obscenity. The works of Chaucer, Smollette, Sterne, Fielding, and Swift, however forthright in matters of sex, circulated without legal hindrance. This immunity apparently extended even to pornography unrelieved by literary quality. In 1708 Lord Holt ruled that the notorious "Fifteen Plagues of Maidenhead" would not support an indictment. As late as 1733 there was a like ruling on the salacious poems of the Earl of Rochester.

Queen Victoria ushered in an era which witnessed an unprecedented drive for the purification of literature. Shelley's "Alastor" was attacked as offensive, and Shakespeare was bowdlerized. The morality drive which flourished in England found its counterpart in America. Hawthorne's, "The Scarlet Letter," was called a "brokerage of lust," and Walt Whitman was discharged from the U. S. Department of the Interior because of "Leaves of Grass." "Huckleberry Finn" was banned as "trash and suitable only for slums" because Mark Twain had prefaced the book with the waggish warning that persons attempting to find a moral in it would be banished.

In 1688 England ordered Governor Thomas Dongan not to allow any printing press in New York. In 1754, Daniel Fowle, a Boston publisher, was jailed because it was suspected he had printed remarks derogatory to the members of the Colonial Assembly. It was doubtless this background that prompted the inclusion of the guaranty of free speech and press in almost all state constitutions, and in the first amendment to the Federal Constitution.

The early days of the republic witnessed an era of political calumny rarely paralleled in the history of the world. Bitter rivalry prevailed in politics; defamation was seized upon as an effective weapon for demolishing opponents in public life. The partisan fury culminated in the Sedition Act of 1798. The Federalists, assailed by the Jeffersonians and fearful of losing power, rushed through a law which in effect forbade any criticism of the government on pain of severe penalties. Federalist judges and officials were free to use the statute to oppress their political foes, and they did not hesitate to do so. The Sedition Act cut perilously near the root of freedom of speech and of the press. It doomed the Federalist Party forever.

Colonial America took no legal precautions to ward off the taint of sex. The early Presidents read and apparently liked the bawdy and outspoken works of the early English novelists. Chancellor Kent himself, a dour and strait-laced man, confessed he enjoyed Fielding. Yet obscenity laws sprang up in a few states before the middle of the 19th century; one in Vermont (1821), another in Connecticut (1834), and a third in Massachusetts (1835). The Federal Comstock Laws were enacted in 1873 and forbade the mailing, as well as the interstate transportation and importation of obscene matter.

The uplift movement flourished and spread, Elizabeth Barrett Browning's "Aurora Leigh" was denounced as "the hysterical indecencies of an erotic mind." In 1888 Henry Vizetelly was fined for publishing Emile Zola's "La Terre"; a year later he was fined again and sent to jail for reissuing Zola's "pernicious literature." Thomas Hardy's "Jude the Obscure" encountered trouble in 1895; and when H. G. Wells's "Ann Veronica" appeared in 1909, a group of influential editors and publishers asked the Home Secretary to suppress it. The repeated confiscation of D. H. Lawrence's works, some claim hastened his death. During recent years many other books, among them "The Well of Loneliness" and "Sleeveless Errand" have been suppressed by the authorities in England.

The list of prose works banned during past and present centuries includes Homer's "Odyssey," Cervantes' "Don Quixote," La Fontaine's "Fables," Defoe's "Robinson Crusoe," Swift's "Tale of Tub" and "Gulliver's Travels," Voltaire's "Candide," Fielding's "Pasquin," Richardson's "Pamela," Casanova's "Memoirs," Goethe's "Faust" and "Sorrows of Werther," Gibbon's "Decline and Fall of the Roman Empire," Sterne's "Sentimental Journey," Andersen's "Fairy Tales," Balzac's "Droll Stories," Flaubert's "Madame Bovary," Maupassant's "Une Vie" and "L'Humble Vérité," Stowe's "Uncle Tom's Cabin," Hawthorne's "The Scarlet Letter," Eliot's "Adam Bede," George Moore's "Flowers of Passion," Zola's "Nana," Hardy's "Tess of the d'Urbervilles," Upton Sinclair's "Oil," Cabell's "Jurgen," Lawrence's "Woman in Love," Sinclair Lewis' "Elmer Gantry," and Remarque's "All Quiet on the Western Front," Dante's "La Commedia" and "DeMonarchia," Shelley's "Queen Mab," Rossetti's "Poems," Baudelaire's "Fleurs de Mal," Whitman's "Leaves of Grass," Elizabeth Barrett Browning's "Aurora Leigh" and Swinburne's "Poems and Ballads."

Hundreds of the disciples of Confucius were buried alive for disseminating their master's beliefs. Roger Bacon, whose treatises on alchemy and optics expressed unorthodox views, was accused of witchcraft and imprisoned for ten years. Sir Thomas Malory's "Morte d'Arthur" was attacked as no more than "bold adultery and wilful murder." The church branded Moliere a demon in human flesh for writing "Tartuffe," a satire on religion. Andre Chenier went to the guillotine for "Iambes" and "Jeune Captive." Almost every book setting forth new themes, unfamiliar ideas, or protests against social, economic or religious abuses, met with instant reprisal— Montaigne's "Essays," Descartes' "Meditations," Montesquieu's "L'Esprit des Lois," Swedenborg's "Principia," Rousseau's writings, Kant's "Philosophy," Galileo's study of the Ptolemaic and Copernican theories, Francis Bacon's works, Darwin's "Origin of Species," Marchiavelli's "The Prince," Jefferson's pamphlets, the political works of Thomas Paine and John Stuart Mill, the Koran, the writings of Savonarola, Erasmus, Luther, Tyndale and Calvin. The Bible itself was not immune. Versions of it were suppressed by Emperor

Justinian, the synod of Canterbury, Cardinal Wolsey, the Inquisition, and Queen Mary. In 1525 Tyndale's translation of the New Testament was denounced by the church as "pernicious merchandise" and 10 years later Tyndale was burned at the stake with his books.

It is ironic that the suppressed books in one age in many cases become part of the accepted literature or even the venerated classics of the next. Sometimes the metamorphosis requires generations, sometimes only a few years. Gautier's "Mademoiselle de Maupin" was shocking enough in the middle of the 19th century to deprive him of the wreath of the Academy; in 1922 the highest New York court could find nothing offensive in it. Schnitzler's "Casanova's Homecoming" was suppressed in 1923; it was fully vindicated in 1930. In 1928 a customs court held that Joyce's "Ulysses" was filled with obscenity; in 1934 a higher court found it to be a serious work of art.

The studies of the troublesome Havelock Ellis, once rigorously prosecuted, are now considered standard in the field of sex psychology. Theodore Roosevelt called Tolstoy "a sexual and moral pervert," and the Post Office Department barred his "Kreutzer Sonata" from the mail in 1890; today it is on the shelves of the public libraries.

There are official and semi-official censors. Official censors are those empowered by law to exercise powers of supervision and suppression. They include judges (despite their oft-repeated declarations that it is not the function of the courts to exercise censorship); and administrative officials such as the Postmaster General, the Collector of Customs and licensing authorities. Administrative bodies and officials purport to operate under specific statutes which outline their powers and prescribe the procedure they must follow. The judges interpret and apply the law in cases that come up before them, as where the seller of an "obscene," libelous or seditious book is prosecuted criminally.

Some idea of the activities of official censors may be gleaned from the fact that in 1922, a bookseller was fined $1,000 for placing a copy of the "Decameron" in the mails; that the highest court in the State of New York upheld a conviction based on Arthur Schnitzler's "Reigen"; that the post office has at various times and places denied the use of the mails to such widely differing works as Ovid's "Metamorphoses," ancient Chinese manuscripts imported by the Field Museum, Swedenborg's "Amor Conjugalis" and the official report of the Vice Commission of the City of Chicago. The customs authorities have sought to bar from our shores Aristophanes' "Lysistrata," Defoe's "Moll Flanders," the "Arabian Nights," the "Satyricon" of Petronius, the "Golden Ass" of Apuleius, Rousseau's "Confessions," Gauguin's "Journals," and Krafft-Ebing's "Psychopathia Sexualis."

The semi-official censors are groups that have no specific powers under the law, but have been organized for the express purpose of "moral uplift." The New York Society for the Suppression of Vice, fathered by Anthony Comstock, the Boston Watch and Ward Society, and the Clean Amusement Association of America, belong in this category. Some of these agencies possess limited police powers. They work in cooperation with the authorities, ferret out alleged violations, act as complaining witnesses, and prod the police and the district attorneys. The New York Society claimed that it was responsible for the confiscation of nearly 200,000 books and other printed material running into millions of copies.

Under the system of government in the United States certain spheres of activity are under national control, and others are left to the states. The federal government has exclusive jurisdiction over the mails and interstate and foreign commerce. The Postmaster General sees to it that the mails are not contaminated, and the Customs Bureau bars from our shores whatever material may be thought to imperil the morals of the American people. On the other hand, whatever happens within the confines of a particular state is regulated by the state itself. The line of demarcation between federal and state censors, while clear-cut in theory, is not sharply observed in practice. A book banned at the customs is effectively kept from the people of the states; the decisions of the federal courts on books, plays and films are usually followed by the state courts, and vice versa.

Censorship, in the historic sense, means prelicensing, that is to say, the submission of material to an official person or agency for approval (imprimatur) in advance of publication or presentation to the public. The licensing of motion pictures by state boards of review is an example of this kind of surveillance.

There is a greater peril to books today than at any other time since the invention of the printing press. The peril does not flow from sex censorship, but from the rise of authoritarian power and the attendant regimentation of thought and opinion. If the world turns totalitarian, there may be a holocaust in books beside which Savonarola's Florentine bonfires will pale into utter insignificance. Hitler's Germany lighted the fires of its destruction when it fanned the flames of burning books.

It was my good fortune to have in association during the trial two men of great legal ability; Mr. Speiser and Mr. Bendich.

In his summation Mr. Speiser struck heavy blows for the right of man to portray in words, that which he saw and felt. Mr. Bendich argued the right to speak freely under the Constitution of the United States and its Amendments.

Both arguments are not included solely because of space. Their value nevertheless did much to impress the Court with our position.

J. W. Ehrlich

San Francisco, California
June, 1960

THE PEOPLE OF THE
STATE OF CALIFORNIA
Plaintiff

vs.

LAWRENCE FERLINGHETTI
Defendant

HON. CLAYTON W. HORN
Judge

FOR THE PEOPLE: THOMAS C. LYNCH
                   District Attorney
                   BY: RALPH McINTOSH
                   Deputy District Attorney

FOR THE DEFENDANT: J. W. EHRLICH
                   LAWRENCE SPEISER
                   ALBERT BENDICH

WITNESSES FOR THE PROSECUTION

RUSSELL WOODS: Police Officer, City and County of San Francisco.

DAVID KIRK: Professor of English, University of San Francisco.

GAIL POTTER: Teacher.

WITNESSES FOR THE DEFENSE

MARK SCHORER: Professor of English, and Chairman of Graduate Studies in English—University of California. Author.

LUTHER NICHOLS: Book Editor, San Francisco Examiner.

WALTER VAN TILBURG CLARK: Professor of Language Arts—San Francisco State College. Taught creative writing at Stanford University, University of Iowa, University of Montana, University of Nevada, etc., etc.

LEO LOWENTHAL: Professor of Speech, Professor of Sociology— University of California.

KENNETH REXROTH: Author, Editor, and Book Reviewer for The New York Times, The Nation, Herald Tribune, and the San Francisco Chronicle.

MARK LINENTHAL: Assistant Professor of Language Arts—San Francisco State College.

HERBERT BLAU: Associate Professor in the Humanities and Language Arts, San Francisco State College.

ARTHUR FOFF: Associate Professor of Language Arts, San Francisco State College.

VINCENT MC HUGH: Author.

THE TRIAL

The Court: Gentlemen, you may proceed.

RUSSELL WOODS, a witness called on behalf of the people, being first duly sworn, testified as follows:

DIRECT EXAMINATION BY MR. MC INTOSH

Mr. McIntosh: Q. State your name.
The Witness: A. Russell Woods.
Q. You are a police officer in the City and County of San Francisco?
A. Yes, sir.
Q. Calling your attention to May 21st, 1957, did you have occasion to go to the premises located at 261 Columbus Avenue, here in San Francisco?
A. Yes, sir.
Q. Whom did you go there with, Officer?
A. Officer Thomas Pagee.
Q. And what type of premises are those?
A. That's the City Lights Bookshop, a book store.
Q. Who did you see there?
A. I saw the clerk, Shigeyoshi Murao.

Q. And did you do anything there?

A. Yes, sir, I did.

Q. What?

A. I purchased a copy of a booklet entitled, "Howl and Other Poems."

Q. All right. Is this the book that you purchased there (*indicating*)?

A. Yes, sir.

Mr. McIntosh: Just for the moment, Your Honor, may it just be identified?

The Court: People's One for Identification.

Q. Did you have any conversation with Mr. Murao?

A. No, I did not, other than asking him for a copy of "Howl," which he gave to me and received my money—seventy-five cents.

Q. Was he the only one on the premises at the time?

A. Yes.

Q. And you obtained a warrant for Mr. Ferlinghetti's arrest?

A. Yes, sir.

Q. You determined that he was the owner of the City Lights Bookshop, is that right?

A. Yes, sir.

Q. Did you read this book of "Howl," after you purchased it?

A. Yes, sir.

Mr. McIntosh: I see. I'll ask that the book be offered in evidence at this time.

The Court: All right. The book is admitted and may be marked People's One in evidence.

Mr. McIntosh: Now, you may cross-examine.

Mr. Ehrlich: May we have permission to reserve cross-examination of the witness until such time as your Honor has read this book? There are certain motions and objections we desire to make after your Honor has read the book.

It will be of no value to commence cross-examination today or to put in a defense, assuming that we should determine to do so, unless and until your Honor has read the book. Then we can call your attention to various parts. I have in mind that the matter may terminate on the presentation of this book.

The Court: Do you intend to make your motions before you go into the cross-examination of this witness, or just what do you plan?

Mr. Ehrlich: It is our present intention to make our motions before the cross-examination. Some of the motions must be necessarily made at that time; others can be made after we cross-examine.

The Court: In other words, as I understand it, some of your motions will be directed toward the contents of this book?

Mr. Ehrlich: Some of them will.

The Court: All right. What's your position, Mr. McIntosh?

Mr. McIntosh: Well, Mr. Ehrlich and I have discussed this matter and I have no objection. You have the book before you. Naturally, you will have to read it to determine whether or not it is obscene and or indecent. And then, of course, we could continue on after you have read it just like we stopped at this moment, and he could make his cross-examination and make his motions if they are proper at that time.

The Court: I certainly would have a better understanding of what is before me after I read the book. I have not read it or seen it until today and I would be in a better position to understand the nature of the motions and the nature of the cross-examination, if any. The matter will be continued until August the 22nd at 2.00 P.M. for further hearing.

The Court: Are you ready, Gentlemen?

Mr. McIntosh: The people are ready, your Honor, but I

understand the defense is waiting for their eminent counsel
Jake Ehrlich.

What I wanted to read into the record, your Honor, is
not very much, but it is pertinent to our case. I want to show
on the first page inside of "Howl" it says: "The Pocket
Poets Series, Number Four, City Lights Pocketbook Shop,
San Francisco." And on the second page it reads: "The
Pocket Poets Series, Published by the City Lights Pocketbook Shop, 261 Columbus Avenue, San Francisco, Calif.,
and distributed nationally by the Paper Editions Corpora-
tion, manufactured in the United States of America." However, on the following page, way down at the bottom, is:
"All these books are published in heaven." And I don't quite
understand that, but let the record show anyway, your Honor,
it's published by the City Lights Pocketbook Shop.

People's case, your Honor.

Mr. Ehrlich: Your Honor, the defendant now moves the
Court for judgment that the publication is, one, not obscene,
and two, that the defendants be found not guilty. We are prepared to argue for such judgment and, if your Honor desires
it, to submit a written memorandum covering the various
points involved.

The record establishes that a police officer entered the
bookshop and bought "Howl." The defendant is charged
with the violation of Section 311, which provides: "Every
person who wilfully and lewdly—" "either—" and I skip to
subdivision 3 of that Section—"writes, composes, stereotypes,
prints, publishes, sells, distributes, keeps for sale or exhibits
any obscene or indecent, writing, paper or book, etc."

I assume your Honor has now read the book. The question
then arises whether as the result of your reading you have
been able to form judgment as to whether this book is or is
not obscene. In addition your Honor must not only determine what is the law as it is applicable to this issue, but you
are to determine whether this book is an obscene book. If

your Honor determines that the book is not obscene under the law, then, of course, that's the end of the issue.

There is yet another step, assuming for the sake of this argument only, that your Honor after reading this book has come to the conclusion that it is obscene. Then we are confronted with the second part of the description of the crime—whether the sale was wilfully and lewdly made.

There is nothing in the record showing any discussion or conduct on the part of the defendant other than selling the book. Now, let's see what is on the cover—"The Pocket Poets Series, Howl and Other Poems, Allen Ginsberg, introduction by William Carlos Williams, Number Four." Let us stop with the cover. Is there anything about this book that indicates that there is something in it that will destroy the moral tenor of the community or do anything which would lead to a moral breakdown of the people of this City, to say nothing of Police Officer Woods?

The question is whether the community will be affected by it. So, your evaluation of the contents of this book must be made in the light of the community feeling about matters of this kind. I have looked at Mr. McIntosh's copy. He has underscored some words. I believe your Honor will agree with me that individual words in and of themselves do not make obscene books, and if it becomes a question of what the words mean, particularly some, I am ready, willing and able to define them. Some people think that certain four-letter words in and of themselves destroy mankind from a moral standpoint. This, of course, is not the law. There was a time, your Honor, when words which today are frowned upon, were in common usage, were not considered improper and were used daily by decent people.

We are confronted with the manner in which this book is to be evaluated by the court. As I understand the law, the court must construe the book as a whole. I presume that I could take the classic, "Leaves of Grass," and by cutting it to pieces find a word here or there or an idea that some people may not like. But in "Leaves of Grass," there is the intent of the poet to convey a certain idea, not lewd and lascivious or licentious or common, but a story, laying out a certain format concerning life itself.

Your Honor probably recalls that it hasn't been too many years ago when the word, "syphilis," was considered improper for use in so-called proper society, and it was not until we found an instant cure for this disease, that we commenced openly discussing this terrible affliction for mankind. We delete words when we believe people are offended and not because of the words per se.

Referring to the matter of content for a moment, I call your Honor's attention to the Wepplo case, which is particularly cited in Roth versus United States. I read from People versus Wepplo:

"Since section 311, Penal Code, condemns the sale of a book, rather than a part of a book, we agree with the contention that a book must be considered as a whole in determining whether this law is violated. On this subject we agree with these statements made in Commonwealth versus Isenstadt: 'It is not to be condemned merely because it may contain somewhere between its covers some expressions which, taken by themselves alone, might be obnoxious to the statute. But this does not mean that every page of the book must be of the character described in the statute before the statute can apply to the book. It could never have been intended that obscene matters should escape proscription simply by adjoining to itself some innocent matter. A reasonable construction can be attained only by saying that the book is within the statute if it contains prohibited matter in such quantity or of such nature as to flavor the whole and impart to the whole any of the qualities mentioned in the statute, so that the book as a whole can fairly be described by any of the adjectives or descriptive expressions contained in the statute. The problem is to be solved, not by counting pages, but rather by considering the impressions likely to be created. For

example, a book might be found to come within the prohibition of the statute although only a comparatively few passages
contained matter objectionable according to the principles
herein explained if that matter were such as to offer a strong
salacious appeal and to cause the book to be bought and read
on account of it.' "

There is nothing in the record to indicate that "Howl,"
was purchased for its content. Nor is there any evidence before this court that any representation was made concerning
the contents of the book, nor is there any evidence before the
Court that in making the sale the purpose of the sale was the
selling of a salacious, lewd or indecent book.

Reading again from the Wepplo case:

"The defendants further contend that the Court erred in instructing the jury on the matter of intent and in excluding
evidence regarding it, and that the evidence fails to show such
intent as is necessary to constitute the offense charged. These
contentions must be sustained."

Specific intent cannot be inferred; it must be proved.
There is not one word in the record going to the intent of
this defendant in the sale of this book. Again, I am saying
nothing about the contents. As a matter of law, the prosecution has failed to establish a case.

And now referring to a very important case in California,
your Honor, Bates versus Newman, 121 Cal. App. (2) at page
800. In that case the plaintiff was suing a doctor whom he had
retained to operate on him. He had been advised by his in-
ternist that he needed what is commonly known as circum-
cision. The doctor performed the operation and as a result of
the operation certain alleged injuries were pleaded by the
plaintiff as against the doctor. The case was tried before a
jury and was finally decided by the Appellate Court. In that
decision the following paragraph appears:

"Patient in the office. Examination of the penis shows complete healing and the patient has more shaft exposed than he ever had available for intercourse before surgery. Whether his personal anatomical conformation will permit his insertion of penis for intercourse is a doubtful matter to me."

Is it against the laws of decency for our District Court of Appeal to write of the sexual organ and the sexual act? Was our State and its people destroyed?

The discussion of sex and fornication directly is not considered by our Appellate Court to be outside the realm of decency. The trial jury did not consider the subject indecent. Then how in the name of everything that's holy to the law itself, can this poem create the questionable moral furor steamed up by this arrest?

I ran across one of Macaulay's greatest lines and I thought it appropriate to this discussion:

"We find it difficult to believe that in a world so full of temptations as this any gentleman whose life would have been virtuous if he had not read Aristophanes and Juvenal will be made vicious by reading them."

Isn't that what this case amounts to?

Now, going to the Roth decision, decided just two months ago by the Supreme Court of the United States. In that case the problem before the trial court was certain pornographic books, advertising, soliciting, mailing, and selling, to encourage buying of certain books by describing their content. The question was whether it was a violation of the First Amendment or the Fourteenth Amendment to the United States Constitution. There the United States Supreme Court approved the following instruction to the jury:

"The test is not whether it would arouse sexual desires or sexual impure thoughts in those comprising a particular segment

of the community, the young, the immature or the highly prudish or would leave another segment, the scientific or highly
educated or the so-called worldly-wise and sophisticated indifferent and unmoved. The test in each case is the effect of the
books, pictures or publication considered as a whole, not upon
any particular class, but upon all those whom it is likely to
reach. In other words, you determine its impact upon the average person in the community. The books, pictures and circulars
must be judged as a whole, in their entire context, and you are
not to consider detached and separate portions in reaching a
conclusion. You judge the circulars, pictures and publications
which have been put in evidence by present day standards of
the community. You may ask yourself does it offend the common conscience of the community by present-day standards. In
this case, ladies and gentlemen of the jury, you and you alone
are the exclusive judges of what the common conscience of the
community is, and in determining that conscience you are to
consider the community as a whole, young and old, educated
and uneducated, religious and the irreligious, men, women and
children."

And Mr. Chief Justice Warren in his concurring opinion
says:

"The line dividing the salacious or pornographic from literature or science is not straight and unwavering. Present laws
depend largely upon the effect that the materials may have
upon those who receive them. It is manifest that the same object may have a different impact, varying according to the part
of the community it reached. But there is more to these cases.
It is not the book that is on trial; it is a person. The conduct of
the defendant is the central issue, not the obscenity of a book
or picture. The nature of the materials is, of course, relevant as
an attribute of the defendant's conduct, but the materials are
thus placed in context from which they draw color and character. A wholly different result might be reached in a different
setting."

I conclude with the question whether after reading this book, your Honor has come to the conclusion, one, that it is or is not obscene, and if obscene, what further proof there must be by the prosecution. If your Honor comes to the conclusion that this book is not obscene, that's the end of the case. Anticipating a reply from my opponent, I submit the matter. Of course, if it is necessary to reply, I shall have that opportunity, your Honor.

The Court: Mr. McIntosh?

Mr. McIntosh: Well, this trial is very unusual in its effect, your Honor, that before the defendant's case is in, before the matter is submitted to you, we are coming to the matter of arguing our case. However, as it may be, I might point out these few things: Mr. Ehrlich has forgotten that that particular section of our code, 311.3, also uses the words, "obscene or indecent." Now, I haven't run across much law on this, your Honor, but I take this position, that although some writings which are obscene would be also indecent, not everything which is indecent would be obscene. And I have definitions and I would like to supply them to your Honor. He asks you to look at the book and determine whether it's obscene, but your Honor could also find that the book could be indecent and also come within the purview of Section 311.3.

The Court: Not under the decisions.

Mr. McIntosh: Well, I'll point them out to you. Both decisions under the definitions of words are not entirely different, and you know under our rules of pleading in the State of California, that we have to plead in the conjunctive rather than in the disjunctive and the wording of the code is in the disjunctive and naturally in our complaint we have to plead in the conjunctive. And so, we could either prove that they are obscene or that they are indecent.

The Court: Well, the same section was involved in the Wepplo case and the Wepplo case was reversed among other things becauses the instruction on that very subject was incorrect.

Mr. McIntosh: Your Honor, it went—what I am going to take up later with reference to Mr. Ehrlich's second objection on the point of being sold lewdly, that was the instruction in that case.

The Court: I won't interrupt any more; you go right ahead.

Mr. McIntosh: Yes, sir. This question as to indecent didn't come up at all in the Wepplo case, your Honor. It went off on the point whether or not the books in question had been lewdly sold—specific intent—but I might point out to your Honor that obscene and indecent has several different meanings and it doesn't have the particular meaning ascribed to it by Mr. Ehrlich. In People versus Wepplo, of course, the Court said that the book was obscene if it had a substantial tendency to deprave or corrupt its readers by inciting lascivious thoughts or lustful desires and quotes the language from Commonwealth versus Isenstadt, which Mr. Ehrlich has also read you a portion of and which I have here. In a summation of many cases, 67 Cal. Jur. Second, page 19 states that:

"The word 'obscene' is variously defined as meaning offensive to modesty or decency or chastity; offensive to the senses or to taste or refinement; characterized by, or given to, obscenity; expressing or suggesting unchaste or lustful ideas; expressing or presenting to the mind or view something which delicacy, purity, and decency forbid to be exposed; tending to stir the sex impulses or lead to sexually impure and lustful thoughts; tending to corrupt the morals of youth or lower the standards of right and wrong, specifically as to the sex relation. The term is further defined as signifying something that is foul or filthy, and for that reason offensive to pure-minded persons; something suggestive of lustfulness, lasciviousness, and sensuality; licentious and libidinous and tending to excite feelings of an impure or unchaste character. The word 'obscene' is also defined as meaning abominable, disgusting, filthy, foul, impure, indecent, lewd, loathsome, ill-looking, repulsive, and unchaste."

In Gore versus State, 54 Southeastern (2), page 669, a Georgia appellate case, your Honor, we also cite the definition:

"The word 'obscene' as used in statutes making the possession or exhibition of 'obscene' pictures, etc., a felony, means not only language suggestive of sexual intercourse, or tending to excite lewdness, or to debauch the public morals, but means offensive to the senses, repulsive, disgusting, foul, filthy, offensive to modesty or decency, impure, unchaste, indecent or lewd."

Now, in reference to indecency. Although there are a lot of courts that do consider that the words are synonymous I think that even you and I will agree, leaving out the exact legal definitions, that something—some things which might be indecent would not be also obscene or lewd. It's a little shading, in the meaning, your Honor, and I have a definition here—

The Court: May I interrupt you? You are flying in the face of the First Amendment, freedom of the press and speech. The Supreme Court in the Roth case held that the exception to freedom of speech under the First Amendment was obscenity, and it limited it to obscenity. It didn't include anything else; it didn't even refer to anything else like indecency or anything of that sort. In other words, they stopped at the line of obscenity.

Mr. McIntosh: The point was not raised in that court, your Honor. They used the word but didn't follow and say anything about indecency.

The Court: Well, they very definitely made it clear. Many of the judges felt that even the word obscene—or obscene writing should be protected by the First Amendment. And your Roth case was actually a five-to-four decision. So, I think I can stop you right there as far as "indecent" is concerned. This Court feels that it will follow the Roth decision as the basis of what may or may not be the subject of an exclusion or exception to the First Amendment, and these books are either obscene or not obscene. I am not going to quibble about the word "indecent" or even consider that it is something lesser than obscene. It either has to be obscene or not.

Mr. McIntosh: Very well, your Honor. Going on to Mr. Ehrlich's second point, in reference to People versus Wepplo, I have had it quoted in many, many cases to the effect that the books had to be lewdly sold. He said there's no evidence in this particular case to show that the defendant lewdly sold the book. Now, of course in the Wepplo case, which Mr. Ehrlich read, it said that the lewd intent may be proved by knowledge of the character of the writings themselves. I don't know whether Mr. Ehrlich read this part of it to you or not, but for the record I will read it.

> "Respondent argues and the trial court apparently believes that this court gave a different construction to this statute in People versus Fananstein, Criminal Appeal 1995, an unpublished decision. That case also involved a prosecution for violation of subdivision 3 of 311 of the Penal Code, and in the opinion affirming a conviction, this Court, after stating one of the defendant's arguments to be that the evidence was insufficient to show that he lewdly kept obscene writings, papers or books for sale, went on to declare this rule in regard to it: 'One who keeps for sale obscene or indecent writings, papers, or books, knowing the character thereof, acts lewdly in so doing because the sale of such 'literature' tends to demoralize those into whose possession the same may come.' Following this statement, this Court said that Section 311 should be liberally construed to effectuate its purpose of stopping the circulation of obscene or indecent 'literature,' and that any other interpretation of subdivision 3 'than that here given would have the practical effect of nullifying that subdivision.' This is no ruling that a lewd intent need not be proved in order to establish a

violation of subdivision 3 of Section 311, but rather a holding that the character of the writings, etc., which he kept for sale, and that from such knowledge a lewd intent might be inferred."

Now, I want to state this, your Honor—

The Court: May I interrupt you and direct your attention to this language in the Wepplo case:

"Where the statute makes a specific intent an element of the offense, such intent must be proved. Of course, the proof may be, and, on the part of the prosecution in most cases, it is, circumstantial; but, if so, the circumstances must be such as reasonably to justify an inference of the intent. Here the facts proved were merely that the book was in stock in the bookstore owned by one of the defendants and was, on request,"—

same situation here—

Mr. McIntosh: Yes, your Honor.

The Court:

"Sold by the other defendant to a police officer. The book was introduced in evidence, but it bears no marks or indications of its character on the outside, nor is its title enlightening or even suggestive on the subject. This evidence, without more, is not sufficient to show that defendants 'lewdly' sold the books. If it appeared that the defendants knew the obscene character of the books, this would support an inference that they acted lewdly in selling it, but we find in the record no evidence to this effect. The defendant Eastman, who sold the book but did not own the store,"—

Well, that has something on intent. Now, can you point to me before you go on anything in the record which is different from this case in the Wepplo case?

Mr. McIntosh: Yes, your Honor. In this case we have in the record that Mr. Ferlinghetti was the owner and publisher of this particular place. People's Exhibit No. One so definitely states. Now, under State versus Holdeger, in 15 Washington, 46 Pacific 652, there a defendant was indicted for knowingly printing, selling, etc., an obscene and indecent newspaper. On the question of knowledge, the Court said,

> "If one can edit and compose a publication without knowledge of its obscene character being conclusively presumed, then it would be idle to allege knowledge of its obscene character because there would be no way of proving that it had such knowledge. Such knowledge must be conclusively presumed from the fact of his composing and editing the publication."

Your Honor, the inference is in this case—I wouldn't go so far as to say it is conclusively presumed because I don't think that is fitting, but certainly if this was before a jury I'd ask for an instruction that an inference be drawn by the mere fact the publisher publishes something, he must have knowledge of what he's doing.

The Court: Your position is, I take it, then, the same as that presented by Mr. Ehrlich, that there is nothing on the outside of "Howl"—

Mr. McIntosh: I stipulate to that, your Honor, nothing obscene about it. And I might say further, your Honor, anticipating something else, that the salesman had no knowledge of what was in the book; purely a salesman like in the Eastman case.

The Court: Now, I take it, then, going back to the salesman, that you agree that there is nothing in the record showing that he has read these books or knew their contents or that there was any lewd intent on his part in selling them?

Mr. McIntosh: That is correct, your Honor. Now, I might say this, though, first: It's a sad commentary on a deal of this kind that counsel should hide behind technicalities. Some of our United States cases are "The United States versus Book, and so forth," and some of the cases do say we are trying the man rather than the book, and if we throw these cases out on technicalities, it will just mean retrying the cases later on to determine whether or not the book is obscene or not.

The Court: I am merely trying to narrow the issues, not trying to pin you down to any particular point.

Mr. McIntosh: Well, I am not going into this argument to point out from the pages of "Howl" the lewd passages at the moment, your Honor, because the defense has not presented their case and I think it is inappropriate to argue that point until the defense is in and the case is substantially before your Honor for decision, and I contend that we have, by inference, shown that Ferlinghetti has knowledge of the character of this work, and I say your Honor might, in reading some of the cases, might have a feeling that these words in there are lewd, and if he puts on a defense that he doesn't know that there are such words as are in there, or that these words are not lewd, of course, I don't believe that would be pertinent to the case because, after all, the book stands and falls by whatever your Honor's decision is as to the obscene character of the writings there.

The Court: Now, coming back to the defense motions, which are in effect a motion to dismiss on the ground of the insufficiency of the evidence, the motions will be denied. So, it will be incumbent upon the defense either to submit the case without testimony and argue it, or to present testimony.

Mr. Ehrlich: Our thinking is, your Honor, that as a matter of law, you must first determine whether the book is obscene or not before we have the burden of introducing testimony. What testimony would your Honor receive in this type of a situation? Can the defense introduce evidence of reviewers, critics, literary people, and those who have made a life work of literature? Is it necessary to put into the record the thinking of men, who are instructors in this subject, that they believe after reading—and I quote from Howl—"saw the best minds of my generation destroyed by madness, starving hysterical naked"? What can they add, your Honor, to the testimony in this record by telling you that this is a reflection of the thinking of the writer as he sees this world? Will they say, that the grammar is not exactly what it should be, or will they say that the construction of the poem is not what they think it should be, or will they say they see absolutely nothing immoral or improper in the poem or in the book, or are we going to get to the point where we're going to ask for definitions of words? I must assume that your Honor in construing this book is going to construe it as a book and not on what appears on page 3 or two words on page 27 and a couple of words on some other page.

The Court: That is the rule of construction as laid down by the cases.

Mr. Ehrlich: Yes. You must read the book as a whole. Is it intended to be lewd and lascivious and licentious, and is it intended to create sex desires—lascivious sex desires? Is it going to destroy the community? If your Honor says you want opinion evidence, I am prepared at this time to make an offer of proof.

The Court: Well, you asked a question; I will answer it. I'm not asking for testimony; I am merely pointing out that in my interpretation of the law it is up to the defense now at this state of the proceedings to either present a case, which they may or may not do in their judgment, or to submit the matter.

Mr. Ehrlich: I have before me on the letterhead of the University of California, the Department of English—

Mr. McIntosh: I am going to object to going into this sort of thing.

The Court: This, I understand, is an offer of proof.

Mr. McIntosh: All right, well, are we going ahead, then?

Mr. Ehrlich: I haven't said yet. I want to argue my point, then we will determine it, if I may, your Honor.

The Court: In substance, what is that you are going to read from, Mr. Ehrlich?

Mr. Ehrlich: It is a statement made by Professor Mark Schorer, who is an instructor in the Department of English of the University of California, dealing with literature, dealing with the reviews of this book, his reading of this book, his construction of what this book says, and I'd be willing to let your Honor read this if you have any objection to my reading it into the record.

Mr. McIntosh: Oh, I certainly have, because the law is all against you, Mr. Ehrlich.

Mr. Ehrlich: I don't understand it that way.

Mr. McIntosh: It is critics deciding an ultimate point of law.

Mr. Ehrlich: It is a matter of discretion with the Court. The Court either may or may not take opinion evidence.

The Court: When were those reviews written, before or after this case originated?

Mr. Ehrlich: These statements are dated August the 16th. And here is a communication from William Hogan, the Literary Editor of the San Francisco Chronicle, referring to his review at the time of publication.

The Court: Well, now, this is what the Wepplo case states apropos of this same subject:

"It may be that some of the book reviews offered by the defendants were relative to the question of intent. If it appeared that the reviews commended the book without disclosing its true character—as apparently some of them did—and that the defendants had read such reviews and relied on them, having no more accurate knowledge in selling the books, these facts would tend to establish a lack of lewd intent."

And then, of course, on the question of whether the books are or are not obscene, book reviews by competent, recognized critics and experts in the field have been used by some of the courts and admitted in order to help the Court arrive at a decision. But letters solicited specifically for the purpose of, you might say, introducing self-serving declarations, or for the specific purpose of exonerating the defendant, of course, would not be admissible.

Mr. Ehrlich: There is no argument about that, your Honor, but the offer of proof would be that if these men were called to testify that they would testify to certain opinions.

The Court: What is your position on my statement, Mr. McIntosh? Do you agree or disagree with it as to the law?

Mr. McIntosh: I disagree, your Honor; not the first part, the Wepplo case you read. The case also goes on further— I believe on page 962, your Honor—to the effect that if a book has literary merit that does not prevent it from being obscene if it otherwise has that character, and gives numerous citations. It says: "It does not appear that the critics whose opinions were offered discussed the question of obscenity, but if they had done so it would have been proper to exclude the opinions because that is the very issue before your Honor."

The Court: Well, I would confine the admission of any testimony, if it were to be admitted at all, to literary critics and experts in that field. As far as sociologists and psychiatrists are concerned, and you can produce a number on both sides to come up here and testify both ways, and from the number of cases and different decisions throughout the United States, it is obvious that you are never going to get unanimous consent on anything that is involved in this case. That's the reason it is such a difficult question. That's the reason why the freedom of the press should be so stringently protected, so that no one segment of the country can censor to the injury of the rest, what they can read, see and hear and so forth. That is why this case is such an important one, why I am giving it such a lot of time and consideration.

Mr. McIntosh: At the moment, though, I don't think we should throw out the Wepplo case. It's been recognized.

The Court: I am not throwing out the Wepplo case. What-ever testimony would be offered would be ruled upon at the time. In other words, I am not going to make a blanket ruling now either one way or another.

Mr. McIntosh: You can see how far this thing could get out of hand, both sides bringing down all kinds of expert wit-nesses and telling your Honor how you should decide when your Honor has your own rules there. I think your Honor can fairly and conscientiously interpret the rules as set down, trying to take an objective view of it through the whole com-munity and decide it yourself.

The Court: For the guidance of counsel, I feel that al-though certain testimony would be admissible, as I have re-lated, that I would not permit the direct question to be asked of such a witness, "Do you consider this book obscene?" be-cause that is something that the Court has to determine. I feel that a legitimate purpose would be served by submitting the book reviews or critics' reviews, even if you wanted to pro-duce a critic or literary expert and propound questions to him such as whether or not—rather, regarding the theme of the book, plot, whether or not the use of certain words are consonant with the theme expressed, and things of that type. But I feel at this moment, unless I am persuaded to the con-trary, that I would not allow such a witness to answer the direct question, feeling that this should be reserved for the Court with the guidance of such people, if any.

Mr. Ehrlich: Would your Honor permit the witness to testify that as a result of his learning and reading and teach-ing in this particular field . . .

The Court: I'm afraid I would have to reserve my decision on that until the question was asked. At the moment, I feel that that's too broad a question to ask.

Mr. Ehrlich: May I approach the matter from another standpoint?

The Court: Unless, of course, there is some direct authority that says such a question may be asked.

Mr. Ehrlich: I don't have any such authority, your Honor.

The Court: I don't recall any, either.

Mr. Ehrlich: All of the decisions of our Appellate and Supreme Courts around the country have avoided that. They have left it a matter of discretion.

The Court: Well, I think the reason for that, Mr. Ehrlich, is that you could produce a hundred people and probably get fifty answers on each side.

Mr. Ehrlich: I am sure of that.

The Court: So I think that question would have to be eliminated unless, as I say, you can show me some direct authority which would allow the asking and answering of such a question.

Mr. McIntosh: The prosecution rests.

The Court: Let the record show that the prosecution rests. This is the opening for the defense.

Mr. Ehrlich: The defense calls Mr. Schorer.

MARK SCHORER called as a witness on behalf of the defense, being first duly sworn, testified as follows:

DIRECT EXAMINATION BY MR. EHRLICH

Q. Your name, place of residence and occupation, please.

A. Mark Schorer, 68 Tamalpais Road, Berkeley, California. I am a teacher and a writer.

Q. Where do you teach?

A. At the University of California. I am professor of English and chairman of graduate studies in English.

Q. Tell us, Professor, whether you have done any writing, and if so, of what nature?

A. I have published three novels, about 75 short stories,

32 of them collected in one volume, more pieces of literary criticism than I know the number of, in practically every periodical one might name.

Q. Did your writing include articles of criticism of other men's work?

A. Yes.

Q. Do you mind naming them for the record, please?

A. No. The first was called "A House Too Old," second, "The Hermit Place," third, "The Wars of Love."

Q. In addition to those three novels, you say you have written a great many articles for magazines?

A. Yes.

Q. Can you presently recall a few of the magazines in which these articles appeared?

A. Well, I am a regular reviewer for The New York Times Book Review; I have published in the so-called literary quarterlies, "Kenyon Review," "Hudson Review," "Sewanee Review," "Partisan Review," "The Reporter"—you want only criticism now?

Q. I am speaking only of criticism.

A. Yes. Well, that's a good sample; most recently in "The Evergreen Review."

Q. Incidentally, does the "Evergreen Review" deal with poetry particularly?

A. Poetry and prose. I was dealing with D. H. Lawrence.

Q. Can you give us anything else concerning your background and learning which I haven't elicited by these questions?

A. I should have said that I have written or collaborated on half a dozen text books for college use, that I am a literary adviser as to publications of the Modern Language Association, a scholarly journal, that I frequently read books for university presses and advise as to publication, the Harvard University Press and Princeton University particularly, a paid consultant of the Army in choosing text books for its educational program.

Q. United States Army, I take it?

A. Yes.

Q. Your work on The New York Times Book Review is given over primarily to criticism?

A. Yes.

Q. Have you in mind presently any particular works which you were called upon to review for The New York Times?

A. You want me to speak particularly of the Times rather than other periodicals?

Q. The Times.

A. I prefer to speak of one of my most recent critical publications.

Q. Very well. What is your most recent?

A. An examination of three texts of D. H. Lawrence's novel, "Lady Chatterley's Lover" in the Evergreen Review, an attempt to collate those texts, and among other things I considered the problem of the alleged impropriety of this work.

Q. Did your criticism of "Lady Chatterley's Lover" take into consideration any of the previous criticism by Anthony Comstock in New York?

A. No. I do not regard that as a serious critique.

Q. You ignored him altogether?

A. Yes.

Q. Are you presently engaged in the writing of any work or article which is of national consequence?

A. I am writing a biography of Sinclair Lewis, whose papers were bequeathed to Yale University. I have been given exclusive access by the executors of his estate. The book will be published in New York and in London.

Q. Have you received any specific honors as the result of the work which you have been doing?

A. Yes. I have had the Guggenheim Fellowship three times; I had a Fulbright award to Italy to pursue my works on D. H. Lawrence and Sinclair Lewis; and I was, last summer, invited to lecture in the University of Tokyo in Japan on another fellowship. I think those are the major honors.

Q. In addition to presently teaching at the University of California, where else have you taught?

A. I have taught on regular academic appointments, at the University of Wisconsin, Dartmouth College, Harvard University, and the University of California. I have also given more incidental courses of lectures in, I suppose, 30 or 35 universities in the United States and also in the University of Pisa in Italy and the University of Oslo in Norway and the University of Tokyo in Japan.

Q. I call your attention to the prosecution's Exhibit One in Evidence. Please tell me whether you have had occasion to read this work?

A. Yes, I have read this work.

Q. Do you have an opinion as to the literary value of Exhibit One, to which we refer as "Howl and Other Poems," by Allen Ginsberg?

A. I think that "Howl," like any work of literature, attempts and intends to make a significant comment on or interpretation of human experience as the author knows it. And to that end he has devised what we would call an esthetic structure to sort of organize his material to demonstrate his theme. The theme is announced in the opening sentence. I don't know it; may I use my own copy?

The Court: Do you want the exhibit to refresh your memory?

A. Yes. The theme of the poem is announced very clearly in the opening line, "I saw the best minds of my generation destroyed by madness, starving hysterical naked." Then the following lines that make up the first part attempt to create the impression of a kind of nightmare world in which people representing "the best minds of my generation," in the author's view, are wandering like damned souls in hell. That is done through a kind of series of what one might call surrealistic images, a kind of state of hallucinations. Then in the second section the mood of the poem changes and it becomes an indictment of those elements in modern society that, in the author's view, are destructive of the best qualities in human nature and of the best minds. Those elements are, I would say, predominantly materialism, conformity and mechanization leading toward war. And then the last part is a personal address to a friend, real or fictional, of the poet or the person who is speaking in the poet's voice—those are not always the same thing—who is mad and in a madhouse, and is the specific representative of what the author regards as general condition, and with that final statement the poem ends.

This is, of course, only the first of the poems, that is, the title poem, but I believe it's the one under chief consideration. So that you have there an organized form to which the poet has devoted himself and through the use of—in order to make an indictment, a social criticism, if I may say so, of certain elements in modern life that he cannot approve, to that end he uses the rhythms of ordinary speech and also the diction of ordinary speech, language of ordinary speech, the language of vulgarity. I think I must stop with that. The language of the street, which is absolutely essential to the esthetic purpose of the work.

Q. So that the use of a particular word, which some think offensive, is necessary to paint the picture which the author tries to portray?

A. Definitely.

Mr. McIntosh: I would object to that as being leading and suggestive.

The Court: I think there is no harm in the question. The objection will be overruled.

Q. After reading "Howl," can you say that the author in his attempt to depict the conditions which he is condemning, has by the use of specific words or otherwise accomplished the purpose which he set out to accomplish?

A. May I rephrase it? Do you mean to ask me whether I think he succeeds in what he wants to do?

Q. Yes.

A. Value judgments are relative. I think he succeeds, yes.

Q. In your opinion are there any phrases or terms used which detract or take away either from the purpose which he is trying to accomplish or destroy the medium which he uses?

A. No. I would say that within his intention, which is a serious intention, the elements that go into the linguistic organization of the poem are all essential.

Mr. Ehrlich: You may take the witness.

CROSS-EXAMINATION BY MR. MC INTOSH

Q. Have you written any poetry, sir?

A. Not since I was a college boy. I have taught poetry, however, for 25 years.

Q. And this "Evergreen Review," that you mentioned, is that the edition for San Francisco which has part of "Howl" in it?

A. No. My essay appeared in number one; the one you are referring to is number two.

Q. Number two has "Howl" in it, is that right?

A. Is it all there? I am not sure. Certainly some of it is.

Q. First part I mean. Now, just what do you mean by literary value?

A. I mean whether the author seriously intends to make a significant comment about experience.

Q. Whether he seriously intends, is that it?

A. Or I could say sincerely.

Q. Well, would you call a book, a poem that is written

one day with a serious purpose must be cast aside, we'll say, in two months, of literary value?

A. One can't predict literary history. What will happen to that poem in twenty years, who knows?

Q. You are not answering the question, sir.

Mr. Ehrlich: I submit he has answered it.

The Court: I think the witness has answered the question.

Mr. McIntosh: Q. Well, what I'm getting at—I don't believe it is too obtuse. Would you say that a book, we'll say, was written seriously at one moment . . .

A. Yes.

Q. . . . but had no particular appeal to anybody, would you say that it had any literary value even though it is written with seriousness?

A. Very great writers, as history has later revealed, had no audience in their own time. The only way I can answer that—

Q. I don't want to go into any double-talk with you. I am asking you whether a book written seriously, where its language is not interesting, we'll say, and perhaps nobody even looked at it, would you call it of any literary value?

The Court: I don't think that question is fair to the witness. I will, Mr. McIntosh, show you where that question is unfair. Suppose I decided—I felt that I was a pretty good author and I wrote a book and I was serious about it and my writing was atrocious, no one ever saw the book. How can you ask the witness whether or not that's any good?

Mr. McIntosh: Well, would you consider it of literary value? That is all I want to find out.

The Court: I know, but that question is not only unfair, but it is not founded on any autoptic profert that the witness can seize upon.

Mr. McIntosh: Q. Well, would you say that "Howl" has any literary merit?

A. Yes.

Q. I presume it was brought to you by counsel or one of his emissaries to read?

A. I bought it first at the U. C. Book Corner in Berkeley.

Q. And I presume you understand the whole thing, is that right?

A. I hope so. It's not always easy to know that one understands exactly what a contemporary poet is saying, but I think I do.

Q. Well, let's go into some of this. You have the book there. Will you open to page 133?

A. Yes.

Q. Well, about the third line down, you understand what "angel-headed hipsters burning for the ancient heavenly connection to the starry dynamo in the machinery of night" means?

A. Sir, you can't translate poetry into prose; that's why it is poetry.

Q. What are "angelheaded hipsters?"

A. That's a figurative statement of "angelheaded"—I would say characters of some kind of celestial beauty like an angel; "hipsters" is part of the vernacular today. I'm not sure I can translate it into any literal way, though.

Q. In other words, you don't have to understand the words to—

A. You don't understand the individual words taken out of their context. You understand the whole impression that is being created and in this first part particularly, where I have already used the word surrealist to describe it. You can no more translate that back into logical prose English than you can say what a surrealistic painting means in words, because it's not prose. Poetry is a heightened form of language through the use of figurative language and rhythm, sometimes rhyme.

Q. Each word by itself certainly means something, doesn't it?

A. No. The words mean only in their context, I would say, and I can't possibly translate, nor I am sure, can anyone in the room, translate the opening part of this poem into rational prose.

Q. That's just what I wanted to find out.

A. It cannot be done, nor can it be done with any poetry. A sonnet of Shakespeare's cannot be translated into rational prose without becoming an entirely different thing.

Q. Well, are there any of these paragraphs which you can translate for us so I can understand it?

The Court: By "translate," do you mean translation into prose?

Mr. McIntosh: Well, so I can understand what the author is getting at.

The Court: Well, the witness just said that you couldn't translate it into prose. Do you mean interpretation or translation.

Mr. McIntosh: Translation—"Who got busted in their public beards returning through Laredo with a belt of marijuana for New York." What does that paragraph mean?

The Court: What paragraph are you referring to now?

Mr. McIntosh: Nine on page 133.

The Court: What is your question with relation to that?

Mr. McIntosh: I asked him what does that mean?

The Witness: I can only put it in my own language, which is not that of the poet, so there is going to be a different thing. I would take the line to mean something like this: Who in their wanderings across the United States all the way from Laredo to New York, probably hopped up, were assaulted— that is not a good word—were injured in their sexual beings. Not very—it is a very pompous paraphrase I am afraid.

Q. Skip down a couple of lines there: "With dreams, with drugs, with waking nightmares, alcohol and cock and endless balls." What significance does that have to you?

A. Well, there are uprooted people wandering around the

United States, dreaming, drugged—that's clear isn't it? Even their waking hours like nightmares, loaded with liquor and enjoying, I take it, a variety of indiscriminate sexual experience.

Q. Do you understand some of these pages where there are just little dots in there?

A. I think I know the words that were intended.

Q. Let's take page 135.

A. Yes.

Q. Fifth line up: "Who let themselves be—" one, two, three, four, five, six dots—"in the—" three dots—"by saintly motorcyclists, and screamed with joy." What does that mean?

Mr. Ehrlich: I don't know how anybody can answer that; there are no words there. I am serious in this objection, your Honor. The objection is that there are no words printed there. Whatever construction Mr. McIntosh may put on it is the construction that he personally puts on it. He is asking the witness to tell him what those dots mean. It is calling for speculation.

Mr. McIntosh: I am asking what the whole thing means.

The Court: No. It calls for speculation on the part of this witness. The objection will be sustained.

Mr. McIntosh: I didn't ask him to supply, I don't believe, Judge; I didn't mean that.

The Court: Perhaps I misunderstood your question. You asked him what those words were supposed to be or what is meant by those dots and dashes.

Mr. McIntosh: I would like to know what is meant by that paragraph.

Mr. Ehrlich: May I make this point, Your Honor? It is the book as a whole which is to be evaluated either for its literary or any other value, not each line nor each word.

The Court: That's correct, but counsel has a right to cross-examine to ascertain whether or not the statement of the witness is based on the document as a whole, and besides this witness testified that there were certain words used in there, commonly used by the man on the street, which were a necessary part of the interpretation or picture portrayed by the author, and counsel for the prosecution has a right to go into that phase of it to ascertain why he so thinks, or whether or not he has some other thoughts on the particular phase.

Mr. Ehrlich: Does your Honor carry in mind the fact that vacant spaces can be filled by people in any way they want?

The Court: As to the vacant spaces, I have already indicated that I would not allow this witness to speculate as to what the author meant by leaving those vacant spaces. But I believe Mr. McIntosh's question now goes to the entire sentence. I think it would make it clearer for the witness if you read the particular sentence you have in mind and ask the witness for his interpretation, or whatever you want to take, as a whole without supplying anything that is missing in the spaces. Would you reframe your question?

Mr. McIntosh: Q. Well, in reading this "Howl," you have to know what certain words mean, don't you?

A. Yes.

Q. All right. Now then, let's take this next sentence: "Who blew and were blown by those human seraphim, the sailors, caresses of Atlantic and Caribbean love." Now, of course, you know what "blew," and "blown," mean, I hope . . .

A. Yes.

Q. They are words of the street, are they not?

A. I believe so.

Q. Now, are those words necessary to this "Howl?"

A. Those words are words that are intended to represent— let me start over. The essence of this poem is the impression of a world in which all sexuality is confused and corrupted. These words indicate a corrupt sexual act. Therefore, they are part of the essence of the picture which the author is trying to give us of modern life as a state of hell.

Q. In other words, they are necessary then?

A. They are illustrations of the general conditions that he's trying to impress us with.

Q. Getting over to page 141, starting with "Dreams!"

A. Yes.

Q. "Adorations! illuminations! religions! the whole boat-load of sensitive bullshit!" Couldn't that have been worded some other way? Do they have to put words like that in there?

Mr. Ehrlich: I object to the question, your Honor, as to whether the author could have used another term or not. This witness can't testify to that.

The Court: I think it is obvious that the author could have used another term; whether or not it would have served the same purpose is another thing; that's up to the author. The objection is sustained.

Mr. McIntosh: Q. I didn't quite follow your explanation to page 143, "Footnote to Howl." Do you call that the second phase?

A. I didn't speak about "Footnote to Howl." I regard that as a separate poem. It is not one of the three parts that make up the first poem. It's a comment on, I take it, the attitude expressed in "Howl," proper, and I think what it says—if you would like my understanding of it—is that in spite of all of the depravity that "Howl" has shown, all of the despair, all of the defeat, life is essentially holy and should be so lived. In other words, the footnote gives us this state in contradistinction to the state that the poem proper has tried to present.

Q. Well, are some of these words in there necessary to the literary value of the piece of poetry? For example, going down to the second line in the "Footnote to Howl?"

A. I think he is saying every part of human life is holy, and he's not the first one who said it. William Blake, a great poet, said it in the eighteenth century. "All that lives is holy" was his way of saying it, his way of saying the same thing. No matter what part you want to mention is just as holy as any other part because it's human, and this, I say, is very much the essence of this poet's view of life.

Q. This poet's?

A. Ginsberg.

Q. Do you know him?

A. No, only as I infer it from this book.

Q. Did you read the one in the back called "America?"

A. Yes.

Q. What's the essence of that piece of poetry?

A. I think what the poem says is that the "I," the speaker feels that he has given a piece of himself to America and has been given nothing in return, and the poem laments certain people who have suffered at the hands of—well, specifically, the United States Government, men like Tom Mooney, the Spanish Loyalists, Sacco & Vanzetti, the Scottsboro boys and so on.

Q. Is that in there?

A. It is in the book. In other words, that is the speaker associating himself with those figures in American History whom he regards as having been martyred. He feels that way about himself.

Q. Well, "America" is a little bit easier to understand than "Howl," isn't it?

A. I think it's a little more direct, yes.

Q. More direct. There is a little small piece of poetry in there like "An Asphodel." You read those too?

A. Yes.

Q. You think they are in a similar vein?

A. They are very different. Those are what one would call lyric poems and the earlier ones are hortatory poems.

Q. What?

A. Poems of diatribe and indictment, the mood is very different, hortatory.

Mr. McIntosh: That's all.

Mr. Ehrlich: Your Honor, we have other witnesses here,

but this might be a good time to determine once and for all whether we are going to pick individual words and start debates on their meanings or the necessity of their use or their value to the work, whether it adds to or detracts from, whether it creates a literary value or destroys it. Mr. McIntosh has dedicated his entire cross-examination to that phase. Your Honor probably observed that the defense studiously avoided going into the construction of these poems piece by piece. We took it as a general over-all publication in line with your Honor's ruling at the last hearing: I quote:

> "For the guidance of counsel, I feel that although certain testimony would be admissible, as I have related, that I would not permit the direct question to be asked of such a witness. 'Do you consider this book obscene?' because that is something that the Court has to determine. I feel that a legitimate purpose would be served by submitting the book reviews or critics' reviews, even if you wanted to produce a critic or literary expert and propound questions to him such as whether or not—rather, regarding the theme of the book, plot, whether or not the use of certain words are consonant with the theme expressed, and things of that type. But I feel at this moment, unless I am persuaded to the contrary, that I would not allow such a witness to answer the direct question."

The Court: Well, I don't think that I have deviated from the language which you have just read Mr. Ehrlich. I think that on cross-examination the prosecution is entitled to ask certain questions of a witness who testifies to the literary merit of a work. For example, I certainly think the prosecution has a right to ask, "Do you consider certain parts or words of this necessary to the theme expressed?" or along those lines. I think that's legitimate cross-examination and doesn't detract from general outlines of evidence that I set forth and which you read from the transcript.

Perhaps we can resolve it this way: I think the rules that

you are referring to are probably two, the first one being that the book is to be construed as a whole; there is no controversy about that; I don't think even the prosecution will dispute that rule. Number two, whether or not the use of certain words which may in their separate context be considered vulgar or coarse or filthy or disgusting or whatever it might be, whether they are necessary or a part of the theme of the book or whether they, together with passages that may encompass them are just put in there for no purpose at all except to excite erotic or lustful desires. I think that generally is what the decisions hold with regard to constructions.

Mr. Ehrlich: I think that is a fair statement of the law, your Honor. There is no difference of opinion, but I do feel that determining whether Ginsberg was justified in using some particular word is not a question to be determined by this Court or to be determined upon the evidence of any witness. The question isn't whether Ginsberg was justified in his use; the question is the purpose for which it is used and whether it produced a certain idea. As I understood Professor Schorer, he said that it produced a certain idea, that he was using the words of today or, the words of the street; so we have no difference of opinion, your Honor, if we stay with that line of examination. But, if we go into examination of what some particular words mean and whether or not they are necessary, then we are not reviewing the book, we are reviewing whether Ginsberg in his mind was justified in the use of some particular word. Now, how can any witness answer that?

The Court: Mr. McIntosh, I'll hear from you.

Mr. McIntosh: I go along with what your Honor said originally. The way the trials are conducted I have a right to cross-examination at every stage of the proceedings.

The Court: I think I will proceed along the same lines generally that we did with the preceding witness. I will allow cross-examination as to particular words and as to particular parts as to whether or not the witness thinks that these words or those parts are necessarily a part of the theme or the vehicle and consonant with the entire vehicle. I think the prosecution is entitled to cross-examine from that standpoint.

Mr. Ehrlich: But your Honor, not whether the author should or should not have used that word.

The Court: No, no. If I gave that impression you misunderstood me. Whether the author should or should not use another word is up to the author, not up to the Court.

LUTHER NICHOLS called as a witness on behalf of the defense, being first duly sworn, testified as follows:

DIRECT EXAMINATION BY MR. EHRLICH

Q. Your name is Luther Nichols?

A. It is.

Q. You reside where?

A. 2845 Woolsey Street in Berkeley.

Q. What is your business, occupation or profession?

A. I am a book reviewer for the San Francisco Examiner.

Q. Meaning the San Francisco Examiner newspaper?

A. Yes.

Q. Do you conduct or are you interested in any other forms of book review?

A. Yes. I have done other reviews, one for The New York Times. I have done television reviewing, an entirely different form, for television station KQED, a 13-program series for the Northern California Booksellers Association.

Q. Have you done any nationwide radio book reviews?

A. I have appeared twice on "Monitor," which is a nationwide network Sunday radio show.

Q. Have you done any particular work in reviewing books, which have been from time to time at issue, such as Exhibit One for the prosecution here?

A. None have come along during my tenure as a book reviewer.

Q. How long have you been in the work of book reviewing?

A. Nearly three years.

Q. I take it that the book review that appears on the page next to the editorial page in the Examiner, is your daily review column?

A. It is.

Q. I call your attention to the Prosecution's Exhibit No. One, entitled "Howl and Other Poems," by Allen Ginsberg, and ask you if you have seen that before and have you read it.

A. Yes I have.

Q. As a result of your experience in book reviewing, have you formed an opinion as to the literary value of Exhibit One?

A. I have.

Q. What is your opinion?

A. My opinion is that Mr. Ginsberg is expressing his personal view of a segment of life that he has experienced. It is a vagabond one; it's colored by exposure to jazz, to Columbia, a university, to a liberal and Bohemian education, to a great deal of traveling on the road, to a certain amount of what we call bumming around. He has seen in that experience things that do not agree with him, that have perhaps embittered him. He has also seen things at a social level concerned with the atom bomb, and the materialism of our time. In sum, I think it's a howl of pain. Figuratively speaking, his toes have been stepped on. He's poetically putting his cry of pain and protest into this book "Howl."

Q. Do you think this book has definite literary value?

A. I do.

Q. And as to the format in which Mr. Ginsberg has done this work, both as to the context and as to construction, do you believe that his method adds to its literary value?

A. I do. As a matter of fact, I think in a way he is employing the jazz phraseology here and, may I say, I think he is also employing the words he heard in his life on the road and in his various experiences.

Mr. Ehrlich: You may take the witness.

CROSS-EXAMINATION BY MR. MC INTOSH

Q. Have you done any writing yourself, sir? I mean outside of book reviews.

A. No, I haven't.

Q. And have you run across reviews of poetry, books of poetry very often?

A. Yes, I do.

Q. Of this type?

A. Not exactly of this type. I think one of the values of the poem is that it is somewhat unique; it is somewhat different, let's say.

Q. You are familiar with the San Francisco Renaissance, are you?

A. Yes.

Q. Have you read books in that vein, or from that group?

A. I have read very recently Jack Kerouac's Book, "On the Road," which is a prose representation, I think, of this same segment of the American population.

Q. Do you understand most of the words in this book?

A. I think I understand their significance and the general context of it.

Q. I see. Taking on page 135—the 32nd line: "who howled on their knees in the subway and were dragged off the roof waving genitals and manuscripts." Now, do you understand what that paragraph is trying to say, as a part of the howl, I mean, this howl against civilization?

A. Not explicitly. I would say he's attempting to show the

lack of inhibition of the persons he's talking of, the members of his group, you might say.

Q. Well, group of what?

A. Of the younger liberals. The post World War Two generation; those who returned, went into college or went into work immediately after World War Two were perhaps somewhat displaced by the chaos of war and didn't immediately settle down.

Q. Well, do you understand the following sentence? I don't have to read it; you can read it.

The Court: Well, you better read it for the record.

Mr. McIntosh: All right.

Q. "who let themselves b—" bunch of dots—"in the—" three dots— "by saintly motorcyclists, and screamed with joy."

Mr. Ehrlich: Well, your Honor, we are getting right back to—

The Court: I think, Mr. McIntosh, that we have to go back to the basis that the book and its contents are to be construed as a whole. In addition to that, the sentence you just read, as you read it, has nothing in it that smacks or savors of eroticism or vulgar language. Now, it may be unusual language but there's nothing in there that contains either of those elements and certainly I can hold that as a matter of law. Now, if you have any particular words that you think are capable of inducing lustful thoughts or depraving anyone or inciting them to commit depraved acts as a result of reading those particular passages or words, or if you think there are some in there that are vulgar to the point of being pornographic, you may direct the witness to them along the lines that we have previously discussed, as to whether or not they are relevant to the theme and to the vehicle itself. But the question that you have just put will not be allowed because you could go through this book line by line and it would be a waste of time and not relevant to the question that's before the Court, to wit: Is the vehicle or book as a whole obscene?

Mr. McIntosh: Well, I am asking him about that sentence, your Honor, in this vein: There is a lot of dots in there; they must mean something to somebody.

The Court: No. I told you before that no witness will be allowed to speculate on what the author might have put in there. So, the Court will sustain the objection to that question.

Mr. McIntosh: All right.

Q. Now, the next paragraph: "who blew and were blown by those human seraphim, the sailors, caresses of Atlantic and Caribbean love." Now, you understand, of course, what "blew" and "blown" mean?

A. Well, I think they are words that have several meanings.

Q. What meaning do you attribute to the words in this paragraph?

A. I think you can attribute all of those meanings to the words in this context. I think it can at one level mean that they were vagabonds, that they were blown about by natural, literal winds. On the other hand, it perhaps does have a sexual connotation.

Q. In reference to oral copulation, right?

A. Yes, possibly.

Q. Now then, do you find that those words are necessary to the context to make it a work of literary value?

Mr. Ehrlich: I thought we settled that, your Honor.

The Court: Yes. Mr. McIntosh, if you will recall, I said that I would not allow the use of the word "necessary." You may ask the question, "Are they relevant?"

Mr. McIntosh: Q. Are they relevant to make this work of literary value?

A. Yes, I would say so.

Q. Well, if you took those words out of there would that spoil the portrayal?

Mr. Ehrlich: That's doing indirectly what your Honor won't permit him to do directly.

Mr. McIntosh: This man is an expert. He has to speculate.

The Court: No, no. Mr. McIntosh, I'm afraid I can't go along with you on that. Here again we get into the realm of speculation whether the author might have used other or different words, which might adequately have gone along with them. But, nevertheless, he chose these words and whether he could have used others or whether the deletions would destroy the vehicle, you are getting into the realm of speculation there. Objection sustained.

Mr. McIntosh: That is what I am afraid of with this expert witness thing, your Honor, contrary to People versus Wepplo. The expert witness gives an opinion to the book and naturally, opinion is what? Partially speculation, his thought on something, and so I ask him his thoughts on what certain sections mean and I am trying to find out. I thought your Honor had in mind having expert testimony for the purpose of helping the Court to arrive at some decision, not as to obscenity, but as to whether or not these are works of literary merit. And even though you might find they are of literary merit, if you do find that the book could be obscene regardless of literary merit—I know your Honor understands that part of the law.

The Court: That's correct.

Mr. McIntosh: But I thought you wanted also to find out whether experts thought that this book had any literary merit, and, of course, Mr. Ehrlich used the word literary value. That's what we are trying to find out, is it not?

The Court: Well, when you say "that's what we are trying to find out" I'm merely here to listen to the testimony as it is adduced. It is not up to me to suggest what the prosecution should bring out in cross-examination or what the defense should bring out on direct. I have made certain statements merely for guidance of counsel. As your questions come up I will rule on them as far as the admissibility of evidence is concerned, and I have indicated to you that if you have any words or statements in or out of context in the book that you want to present to this witness and whether in his opinion he believes that those are relevant, you may do so, but I think you will have to proceed along these lines.

Mr. McIntosh: All right.

Q. Going down a little further, down to the seventeenth line from the top "who sweetened the snatches of a million girls trembling in the sunset, and were red eyed in the morning but prepared to sweeten the snatch of the sunrise, flashing buttocks under barns and naked in the lake."

The Court: What's your question?

Mr. McIntosh: Q. Now, is that word, "snatches," in there, is that relevant to Mr. Ginsberg's literary endeavor?

A. Yes, I think it is.

Q. Of course, it goes along with the whole paragraph?

A. Yes. I think he's trying to convey an idea of fertility there, among other things, and this is his choice of language to convey that idea.

Q. All right. Next one: "who went out whoring through Colorado in myriad stolen night-cars—" and I don't understand that next—then an "N," period, and a "C" period, comma—"secret hero of these poems, cocksman and Adonis of Denver—joy to the memory of his innumerable lays of girls in empty lots and diner backyards, moviehouses, rickety rows on mountaintops in caves or with gaunt waitresses in familiar roadside lonely petticoat upliftings & especially secret gas-station—" what's that next word?

The Court: Pardon me?

Mr. McIntosh: How do you pronounce that?

Mr. Ehrlich: Solipsisms.

Mr. McIntosh: ". . . solipsisms of johns, & hometown alleys too." It is a little hard to read because there are no commas in the spots where you expect them to be.

The Court: I believe the word "solipsisms," is misspelled in the book.

Mr. Ehrlich: Yes, it is. There is an extra "i" in it.

Mr. McIntosh: Q. Now, are these words relevant to the literary value of Mr. Ginsberg's poetry: "cocksman," about the "lays of girls in empty lots"?

A. Well, as I said before, Mr. Ginsberg is writing of his experiences, which have been on a hobo level at times. He's employing the language that is actually in reality used by hobos, by people of his experiences, hitchhikers, and I think in recounting some of these experiences, mentioning them all in this one stanza, if you want to call it that, the words are valid and necessary if he's to be honest to this purpose. I think to use euphemisms in describing this would be considered dishonest by Mr. Ginsberg.

Q. Now, take page 141. When I say, "lines," I mean stanzas, or whatever you call them. Go down about three, starts in with "Dreams!"

A. Yes.

Q. "Dreams! adorations! illuminations! religions! the whole boatload of sensitive bullshit!" Now, is that term, "bullshit," is that relevant to the literary value of Mr. Ginsberg's work?

A. I would say so, yes. Mr. Ginsberg is angry here. Obviously he is using the term that one might use in anger, again in preference to euphemism.

Q. By the way, Mr. Nichols, how do you define a book that has literary value?

A. There are many tests of literary value. The chief one historically is whether it survives its time, whether it is regarded by a consensus of educated qualified people as ultimately having literary value, as being worth reading for the educated person, as being a contribution to society and to the general education of readers.

Q. Well, then, merely because it's written seriously would you say that that alone would give it literary value?

A. Well, not necessarily.

Q. All right. Now, would you say then that this book "Howl" is worth reading for the educated person?

A. Yes, if he wants to hear a cry from a person who represents a certain part of American life, a certain experience of that life.

Q. Well, would he read it for entertainment value?

A. The word "entertainment," has a large and rather vague meaning. To some I would say it would be entertaining.

Q. Well, to what type of person would you feel that this poem would be entertaining?

A. Well, I would say to one who is familiar with the language and its experiences that Mr. Ginsberg is recording. He is expressing, perhaps, some experience of all of them and it would be entertaining to see in words, to see in his thoughts, an expression of some of the experiences they have had, some of the feelings they've had.

Q. Well, you also said, I believe, literary value sometimes is a book which will survive any test of time. Do you think that Mr. Ginsberg's work will survive the test of time?

A. I have no way of knowing.

Q. I ask you, do you think so?

Mr. Ehrlich: He has no way of knowing, no more than some people thought "Leaves of Grass" was going to survive.

Mr. McIntosh: I'm asking for his opinion, to give us an opinion on that book. He said literary value depends upon surviving the test of time. I want to know if it will.

Mr. Ehrlich: If Luther Nichols can answer that, the Good Lord can use a helper and he ought to be there. How can he tell? I object to the question as calling for a conclusion, not for a man's opinion.

Mr. McIntosh: I am asking for his opinion as an expert.

The Court: He has stated that he has no way of knowing. Now, you may ask him if he has anything to add to that but apparently that's his answer.

Mr. McIntosh: Well, I might call your Honor's attention to the fact that he said it's a work of literary value in response to Mr. Ehrlich's direct question. Now, he said one of the definitions of literary value is whether it lasts, whether it survives the test of time. He says it is a work of literary value. I'm asking him if in his opinion does he think Mr. Ginsberg's work will survive the test of time.

The Court: That does call for the opinion and conclusion and I think it goes beyond an allowable opinion and conclusion.

Mr. McIntosh: Well, your Honor, it's just a reverse play, you might call it.

The Court: Let me ask him—can you answer the question?

The Witness: It calls for a prediction. I don't think my prediction would be any more valid than anybody else's. Here I think the best possibility now in "Howl's" survival is for its value as a bit of literary history. I think this case will draw attention to it. It, perhaps, will have a wider readership than it might otherwise have had, and may go down in history as a stepping stone along the way to greater or lesser liberality in the permitting of poems of its type expression.

Mr. McIntosh: That depends on the way his Honor rules.

The Court: In any event, you have your answer.

Mr. McIntosh: Q. Inasmuch as you apparently cannot say with any exactitude, or that it will survive the test of time, yet you say it has literary value. I believe some other test was —you said if it was worth reading by the educated; I think your answer was, yes, to certain types.

Mr. Ehrlich: Object to that question on the ground it is not stating the answer of the witness.

The Court: Well, you read several things there, Mr. McIntosh. I don't know whether you were summing up and asking a compound question or whether you are breaking this down into the component parts. What are you doing?

Mr. McIntosh: Well, first I am restating what he has more or less stated, that in reference to the term of literary value he said it is a book which survives the test of time.

The Court: I don't think you accurately stated the witness' response to the question of survival.

Mr. McIntosh: If I misstate you, I am sorry; I tried to write it down fairly fast here.

The Court: Just so that there will be no question in the record, you did not correctly state the answer of the witness with regard to survival.

Mr. McIntosh: Let's start in again.

The Court: Now, you better start again and get it straight.

Mr. McIntosh: Q. What is your definition of a book that has literary value?

The Court: Now, he has already gone into that.

Mr. McIntosh: That's what I say; that's what I stated.

The Court: You made a misstatement.

Mr. McIntosh: May I ask him then?

The Court: You made a misstatement of the fact and that is what I was merely calling your attention to.

Mr. McIntosh: Q. Did you not state, Mr. Nichols,—I am sorry; we could have read it back but it takes quite a little time for the reporter to find the notes. Did you not state that one of the tests of a book to have literary value, one of the tests among many would be the test of surviving time?

A. Yes, in part, yes.

Q. We have books that have gone down in history; we have them yet, the books themselves. We all read them. They look pretty dry sometimes, but they are all—they have survived the test of time and we expect to read them in school, is that right?

A. (*Witness nods affirmatively*)

Q. And I believe you gave some other definition of a book that has literary value, is that right?

A. Yes, that's right.

Q. Wasn't one of them that it was something worth reading to the—I believe you said—educated? I'm not positive on that last word, but worth reading to someone, is that it?

The Court: I'm not quite sure where you are going. Are you trying to bring out the answers to these same questions again or are you summing up or what? I'm trying to avoid repetitions here.

Mr. McIntosh: So was I, your Honor, but one of my questions—there was an objection made to it. Your Honor thought that I was not following through.

The Court: Well, so that we are not at cross-purposes here, you are going down the line here covering the same ground that you have previously covered.

Mr. McIntosh: To show that he said those things.

The Court: It's in the record. Why go over it again?

Mr. McIntosh: I wanted to ask a question later on.

The Court: Ask what question later on?

Mr. McIntosh: Well, I asked one, so far, whether it survived the test of time and got an answer that didn't mean anything so far.

The Court: No. You are going over the same ground that has already been covered and you are just wasting time on that because it's all in the record. If you have anything new, you may pursue it.

Mr. McIntosh: Q. Now, taking this "Footnote to Howl." Read that, page 143, sir. Now, this first paragraph has 15 "holy's" in there, "Holy! Holy! Holy!"

"The world is holy! The soul is holy! The skin is holy! The nose is holy! The tongue and cock and hand and asshole holy!" Now, are those last words there, are they relevant to the literary value of Mr. Ginsberg's work?

A. It seems to me they are relevant in that they are part of a contrast he is trying to show there between the things that are conventionally accepted as holy and the things that he, in a Whitmanesque sense, or things that are holy in that they are all part of mankind and part of the world. He's showing that everything is holy within a sense, the sense that he is trying to convey here.

Q. Well, there is another part he says is holy, too; going down a little bit, one, two, three, four, five, six, seven lines down: "Holy my mother in the insane asylum! Holy the cocks of the grandfathers of Kansas!" Now, he uses that word again. Is that necessary to the relevancy of the literary value of Mr.—

The Court: Mr. McIntosh, will you delete the word "necessary" from your question? Reframe it.

Mr. McIntosh: Almost have to write it down. Is it relevant to the literary value of Mr. Ginsberg's work?

A. I would say it's relevant to his purpose.

Q. To his purpose?

A. Yes. Which I have just stated, which is to convey the totality of holiness in his interpretation.

Q. Going back to page 136, when I said I didn't know exactly what he meant in the fifth paragraph from the top of the page, when I cited the capital letter "N," period "C" period. Is that an abbreviation of a state or what does it mean, do you know?

A. I'm not sure just what he does mean.

Q. It has no particular significance to you, does it?

A. No.

Q. Did you read that "Transcription of Organ Music"?

A. Yes, I did.

Q. Is that a work of literary value?

The Court: I take it using the word "value," that is synonymous with "merit."

Mr. Ehrlich: They are interchangeable.

Mr. McIntosh: Mr. Ehrlich used the word. I'm following through on it.

The Court: I just wanted to get your thinking on it.

Mr. McIntosh: Yes, literary merit.

The Witness: Yes, I would say it is of some literary merit.

Q. What is Mr. Ginsberg trying to portray in that piece of poetry?

A. I'm sorry to say, while I have read it, I haven't read it recently enough to give an analytical statement of much value there. As I recall, this is a poem in which he is expressing his individual loneliness and yet his appreciation to the Creator for giving him the poetic spirit that enables him to express his loneliness. He's, in a very broad sense, grateful for the power of poetry and expression.

Q. By the way, have you ever written any book reviews on this book?

A. Not specifically. We did mention the book in an article that was done in the paper on the general problem of censorship of "Howl."

Q. Nothing written by yourself?

A. No I haven't specifically reviewed this book.

Q. I mean, but did you write this other article that you are talking about?

A. Yes.

Q. Did you also read "America?"

A. Yes.

Q. "In America," do you see a word in there, four-letter word, do you?

A. Yes.

Q. Is that relevant to the literary value?

The Court: For the record, Mr. McIntosh, what word are you referring to?

Mr. McIntosh: I will read down to the line:

"America I've given you all and now I'm nothing

America two dollars and twenty seven cents January 17,
   1956.
I can't stand on my own mind.
America when will we end the human war?
Go fuck yourself with your atom bomb.
I don't feel good don't bother me."
Now, the word in there, that four-letter work, is that rele-
vant to the literary merit of Mr. Ginsberg's work?

A. Well, Mr. Ginsberg is trying to—

Q. Will you answer my question?

Mr. Ehrlich: Let him answer it then.

The Witness: I am trying to answer. Mr. Ginsberg is trying to say as powerfully as he can or trying to express as
powerfully as he can his indignation at certain things he sees
taking place in the world today. He is obviously—perhaps one
of our biggest problems is the atom bomb. He's tired of it.
He's sick to the point of saying this. He doesn't want to
temper it by saying it any less softly. He's angry, and when
you are angry sometimes you do use words of this sort. I
would say yes, it's relevant; it's in keeping with the wrath he
feels, with the language that he has used throughout most of
these poems. And, yes, I would say it was relevant to the
literary value of the work.

Mr. McIntosh: That's all.

The Court: Call your next witness.

WALTER VAN TILBURG CLARK called as a witness on behalf of
the defendants, being first duly sworn, testified as follows:

DIRECT EXAMINATION BY MR. SPEISER

Q. Would you give your name and address?

A. My name is Walter Van Tilburg Clark; my address is
43 Molimo Avenue, Mill Valley.

Q. Where are you presently employed?

A. I am presently employed as a Professor of Language Arts at San Francisco State College.

Q. And where had you previously been employed?

A. I had taught previously in English and specifically in creative writing at Stanford, University of Iowa, University of Montana, University of Nevada, and on shorter terms, including summer conferences, lecture trips, a Ford Foundation Tour, things of that sort, at Reed College, University of Oregon, University of Washington, Mills College, the University of Arkansas, the University of Missouri, the University of Wyoming, the University of Utah; there are some others.

Q. How long have you been a professor in English and Language Arts?

A. I have been a professor in creative writing specifically and in college level English for—probably 12 or 14 years.

Q. Are you a professional writer?

A. I am.

Q. And can you name some of the books or other publications that you have authored?

A. Three books, "The Ox Bow Incident," "City of Trembling Lights," and "The Track of the Cat," and a collection of short stories and one short novel, "Watchful Gods," and a very early volume of verse that I would rather not name.

Q. Have any of your publications received any awards?

A. Yes, in 1945 or '6—the first award in the O'Henry Short Story Contest for one of the short stories. Aside from that, a number of pieces have been reprinted in anthologies. They have been overall translated into 21 languages.

Q. Have any of your books been dramatized in any form?

A. Yes, both "The Ox Bow Incident" and "The Track of the Cat" have had experimental stage versions presented and movies made from them.

Q. Major productions?

A. The movies were major productions; the others were made by experimental theaters.

Q. Have you had an opportunity to read "Howl and Other Poems" by Allen Ginsberg?

A. I have.

Q. Have you formed any opinion as to the literary merit of the publication?

A. I have.

Q. And would you give the opinion that you formed based on the experience that you have had, both as a professional writer and as an instructor and professor of English and creative writing?

A. They seem to me, all of the poems in the volume, to be the work of a thoroughly honest poet, who is also a highly competent technician. I have no reason to question in my own mind the feelings, Mr. Ginsberg's sincerity in anything that he has said or the seriousness of his purpose in saying it.

Q. In forming your opinion as to the literary merit of the publication, have you considered some of the phrases and words about which Mr. McIntosh questioned other witnesses prior to your taking the stand?

A. Yes, when I knew that I might appear and have to offer an opinion, I examined the poem not only in a general way, but specifically for the purpose of determining my reaction to what I believe might be expressions or passages in question. I found none anywhere in any of the poems that seemed to me irrelevant to Mr. Ginberg's purpose, and it seemed to me also that there is even esthetically a sound defense to be made for each use of what might be considered a questionable term in the way of the tone desired for the whole volume, particularly for the title poem, the tension, the sense of destruction, the sense—even if we wish that—of depravity that he wished to produce. These are victims, these are a lost generation that he is attempting to produce in that poem, and to give us the sense of the violence, the violence of activity, of the attitudes, of the feelings which destroyed them under the conditions he sets forth, I think he could not have done otherwise than use the language which might have been proper or current for them and bore directly the weight and mode of their feeling.

Mr. Speiser: Thank you. Your witness.

CROSS-EXAMINATION BY MR. MC INTOSH

Q. What is your definition of literary merit, anyway?

A. It's very hard to define. I don't know if this is getting outside of my purview, but I don't know exactly why we have to define literary merit in this particular case.

The Court: Mr. Clark, we appreciate your coming here, but you're here as a witness, not to lecture the prosecution. We will have the question read. If you can't answer the question you may say so, but we're not interested in anything but your answer to the question. Read the question, Mr. Reporter.

(*Record read.*)

The Court: If you can answer the question, you may do so, if you can't answer it, you may say so.

The Witness: Your Honor, I can't answer it without going into repetitions of what has been said before by other witnesses.

The Court: Well, that is all right. Don't refer to what they said, but even if it is necessary for you to repeat what others have said, you may do so.

The Witness: Very well. The only final test, it seems to me, of literary merit, is the power to endure. Obviously such a test cannot be applied to a new or recent work, and one cannot, I think, offer soundly an opinion on the probability of endurance save on a much wider acquaintance with the work or works of a writer than I have of Mr. Ginsberg's or perhaps even with a greater mass of production than Mr. Ginsberg's. I would in the instance of some contemporary writers be quite willing to offer an opinion on the probability of status in time, as with William Faulkner with a great, great number of novels and short stories to his credit. Aside from this test of durability, I think the test of literary merit must be, to my mind, first, the sincerity of the writer. I would be willing, I think, even to add the seriousness of purpose of the writer, if we do not by that leave out the fact that a writer can have a fundamental serious purpose and make a humorous approach to it. I would add also there are certain specific ways in which craftsmanship at least of a piece of work, if not in any sense the art, which to my mind involves more, may be tested.

Mr. McIntosh: Q. Well, in writing a piece of poetry or writing a book, part of the literary merit is that of fitting words together properly, is that right, sir?

A. Right.

Q. And you feel that Mr. Ginsberg has made the proper choice of words in this book to make it one of literary merit?

Mr. Ehrlich: Objected to on the ground that it is without the issues and therefore immaterial.

The Court: Sustained.

Mr. McIntosh: Q. Well, then, Mr. Ginsberg's work is one which you would recommend to others to read, is that right, having literary merit?

The Witness: That would depend upon the reader. To people of adult intelligence and perception, I would not hesitate to recommend "Howl and Other Poems."

Mr. McIntosh: Q. Do you classify yourself as a liberal?

The Court: Now wait a minute.

Mr. Ehrlich: The objection is that it is irrelevant and immaterial, doesn't tend to prove or disprove anything in this case. The word "Liberal" is too vague and uncertain.

The Court: Sustained. "Liberal" is too vague and uncertain; it might mean anything.

Mr. McIntosh: Q. Are you familiar with the San Francisco Renaissance?

A. No, I am not.

Mr. McIntosh: No further questions.

The defense calls Mr. Lowenthal.

LEO LOWENTHAL called as a witness on behalf of the defendants, being first duly sworn, testified as follows:

DIRECT EXAMINATION BY MR. EHRLICH

Q. Your name, address and profession please.

A. I am Leo Lowenthal, my residence is 1214 Contra Costa Drive, El Cerrito, and I teach and write.

Q. Where do you teach?

A. At the University of California.

Q. What are you teaching at the University of California?

A. I am Professor of Speech and Professor of Sociology, teaching courses in literature in society and popular culture.

Q. Have you taught elsewhere?

A. Yes. Before joining the University of California I was for one year a fellow for advanced study at Stanford, and preceding that, 1945, Research Director for the Voice of America, United States Department of State; preceding that I was employed by Columbia University and lecturing at Columbia University; before 1933 I was connected with the University of Frankfurt in Germany.

Q. Well, weren't you also at one time connected with the Bureau of Overseas Intelligence of the Office of War Information?

A. Yes, during the war.

Q. From 1941 to 1945 you were a consultant in the Office of War Information?

A. Yes.

Q. Have you written any works?

A. Yes, I have written several books and monographs during the last 30 years.

Q. Could you give us a few of them?

A. Yes. This year I published a book called "Literature and the Image of Man," which studies literary criticism of serious works. Furthermore, I published this year, together with Marjorie Fisk, my wife, a monograph on the problems of Eighteenth Century English Literature called "Debate over Art and Popular Culture in Eighteenth Century England." Furthermore, I have published during the last few years a number of studies on popular literature in America and the whole problem of censorship of literature, which have been printed and reprinted in various magazines and books. Before that I have done other studies in the field of literature and in the field of communications.

Q. Have you had occasion to read and study the prosecution's Exhibit called "Howl and Other Poems" by Allen Ginsberg?

A. Yes, sir.

Q. As the result of your education, your experience, your work in this field, and your teaching of this subject, have you formed any opinion as to the literary merit of "Howl?"

Mr. McIntosh: Your Honor, I would like to object to this witness' testimony. I don't believe he is particularly qualified as a teacher of sociology. Although he has written books, I don't think that would qualify him to criticize or look at other people's writings, unless he is going to actually be in that type of work.

The Court: I'm not considering his background in sociology, just looking at the other elements that have been adduced here.

Mr. Ehrlich: We didn't go in that subject because your Honor indicated you didn't want that.

The Court: That's right. Do you want to question the witness on voir dire as to his qualifications?

Mr. McIntosh: Yes, just for a moment.

The Court: All right.

VOIR DIRE EXAMINATION BY MR. MC INTOSH

Mr. McIntosh: Q. What degrees do you have?

A. I have a Ph.D., and I have another higher degree in literature and history.

Q. You have made what is a hobby of studying literature?

A. It's not a hobby. I have studied literature and comparative literature and have taught it in German and American Universities.

Q. Frankfurt?

A. Yes. My special field is the relationship of literature to society and I am a student of comparative literature.

Q. I see. When you worked with the Bureau of War Information that had nothing to do with literature?

A. No, very indirectly.

Q. And I assume, though, in writing some of these books you had to read a lot of other books to give a criticism of them, is that right?

A. When I write my books on literature I read particularly the works of writers, of the artists, not other books on them.

Mr. McIntosh: I see. That's all, your Honor.

The Court: All right. For the record, I take it you have withdrawn your objection, then?

Mr. McIntosh: Yes, your Honor.

Mr. Ehrlich: Q. Professor, you haven't just made a hobby of this subject; this has been your life's work?

A. That's correct.

Q. Did you say that you had read the book, "Howl and Other Poems" by Allen Ginsberg?

A. I did.

Q. As a result of reading it and predicated on your learning and your experience and your writing and your teaching, have you formed any opinion as to the literary merit of this work?

A. I have.

Q. What is your opinion?

A. Well, my opinion is that this is a genuine work of literature, which is very characteristic for a period of unrest and tension as the one we have been living through the last decade. I was reminded, by reading this poem, particularly "Howl," which I think is here at issue, of many other literary works as they have been written after times of great upheavals, particularly after World War One, and I found this work very much in line with similar literary works. With regard to the specific merits of the poem, "Howl," I would say that it is structured very well. As I see it, it consists of three parts, the first of which is the craving of the poet for self-identification, where he roams all over the field and tries to find allies in similar search for self-identification. He then indicts in the second part the villain, so to say, which does not permit him to find it, the Moloch of society, of the world as it is today. And in the third part he indicates the potentiality of fulfillment by friendship and love, although it ends on a sad and melancholic note actually indicating that he is in search for fulfillment he cannot find.

Q. In your opinion, Professor, has Mr. Ginsberg in this work used any method which would tend to corrupt people in the sense that we refer to corrupt motives?

A. I cannot discover a trace.

CROSS-EXAMINATION BY MR. MC INTOSH

Q. When did you read this book?

A. About a week ago.

Q. And by whom was it called to your attention?

A. I read about it in the newspapers and some of my colleagues brought it to my attention.

Q. I see. And would you recommend it for reading to the average person?

A. I don't know. If I may ask you, what do you mean by the average person? I cannot answer the question.

Q. Well, that's what we have to determine here. Well, what type of person would you recommend it to?

Mr. Ehrlich: I object to that on the ground—

Mr. McIntosh: All right.

The Court: I think Mr. McIntosh, although similar questions were allowed of the previous witness, that you are stepping on the toes, you might say, of the Court's position in making the determination in this case. The rule is how a book as a whole will affect an average person in the community, taking into consideration the period and time involved.

Mr. McIntosh: I see what you mean.

The Court: To ask this witness the question that you are pursuing would depend upon the decision that the court would have to make.

Mr. McIntosh: I understand that, your Honor. I didn't mean it that way, though.

That's all.

Mr. Ehrlich: Step down. Thank you Professor.

KENNETH REXROTH called as a witness on behalf of the defendant, being first duly sworn, testified as follows:

DIRECT EXAMINATION BY MR. BENDICH

Q. You are Kenneth Rexroth?

A. That's right.

Q. Where do you reside, and what is your occupation?

A. I am a writer and reside at 250 Scott Street, San Francisco.

Q. Could you name some of your writings?

A. The most recent one is called "In Defense of the Earth"; before that I wrote "The Signature of All Things";

"The Dragon and the Unicorn"; "The Phoenix and the Horse"; I think that's enough. I have done books of—three books of translation in print, "A Hundred Poems from the Chinese," "A Hundred Poems from the Japanese," "Thirty Poems from Spanish." I have edited several books, a collection of D. H. Lawrence, and have been editor and editorial adviser for the publishing house of New Directions for a good many years.

Q. In the course of your literary career have you had occasion to engage in the writing of other material than poetry?

A. Well, one of the principal sources of my income is the writing of criticism. I write for The New York Times, the Nation, Herald Tribune, and the San Francisco Chronicle. I have done this almost all of my life.

Q. What is the nature of the writing which you do for The New York Times?

A. Mostly reviews of poetry.

Q. What is the nature of the writing you do for Nation?

A. Very little of that is poetry. It's work of science and scholarship and *belles lettres* of various sorts.

Q. Will you tell the Court whether there is anything in your professional background indicating your capacity as an expert witness in this matter?

A. I'm an American poet of recognized competence, and poetry critic of recognized competence. I have had a couple of Guggenheim Awards and other things and I am, I guess, by now, in most poetry anthologies.

Q. Have you had occasion to engage in critical work in any medium other than the written medium?

A. If you mean do I conduct a radio program on KPFA, yes.

Q. And what, Mr. Rexroth, is the nature of the KPFA radio program?

A. It's a book review program.

Q. I see. Now, Mr. Rexroth, have you had occasion to read "Howl and Other Poems" by Allen Ginsberg?

A. I have.

Q. And in the light of your professional background, how would you identify the nature, the theme of "Howl?"

A. Well, the simplest term for such writing is prophetic; it is easier to call it that than anything else because we have a large body of prophetic writing to refer to. These are the prophets of the Bible, which it greatly resembles in purpose and in language and in subject matter.

Q. How would you describe the theme?

A. Well, the theme is the denunciation of evil and a pointing out of the consequences and a call to repent and a pointing out of the way out, so to speak. That is prophetic literature. "Woe! Woe! Woe! The City of Jerusalem! The Syrian is about to come down or has already, and you are to do such and such a thing and you must repent and do thus and so." And the poem, "Howl," the four parts of the poem do this very specifically. They take up these various specifics seriatim, one after the other.

Q. Do you care to elaborate on that?

A. Well, I would be simply going over the statements made by Doctor Lowenthal. I mean, the first part is a picture of general alienation of one man from another throughout society and particularly throughout the society of youth which has been demoralized by actually two major wars, by the threat of imminent death and by the commercialism, and not just the commercialism, but the particularly predatory elements of the commercialism in modern society. And, of course, the terminology is almost entirely Biblical. Moloch, of course, is a symbol for Hebrew prophets of commercialism and they considered it bestiality of the Philistines. And the third part is the picture of the consequences, the utter demoralization of an individual. Incidentally, I might say the individual, Carl Solomon, is a poet; he actually exists, and at one time was considered to have considerably more talent than Allen Ginsberg himself. And "Footnote to Howl," of course, again is Biblical in reference, the reference is to the Benedicite, which says over and over again, "Blessed is the fire, Blessed is the light, Blessed are the trees, and Blessed is this and Blessed is that," and he is saying, "Everything that is human is Holy to me," and that the possibility of salvation in this terrible situation which he reveals is through love and through the love of everything Holy in man. So I would say, that this just about covers the field of typically prophetic poetry.

Q. Have you had an opportunity to form an opinion as to the literary merit of the work?

A. I have.

Q. Would you state what your opinion is in that regard?

A. Well, it is, of course, impossible to tell what will survive the test of history and what will not and, of course, it's even impossible to tell if history is ever going to judge right. There are many works of great merit that are extremely obscure, known only to scholars, but I would say a work like this, that is a contemporary work and in the field of contemporary poetry, that its merit is extraordinarily high, that it is probably the most—certainly in my opinion—is probably the most remarkable single poem, published by a young man since the second war.

Q. Would you care to specify further your understanding of the criteria of literary merit?

A. Well, again that has been covered by all the other witnesses and I agree with them. I mean, for a work to have literary merit it must have sincerity and seriousness of purpose and should also, I believe, probably have a certain wholeness, which I think that this has. I don't think "Howl" is just a cry of wrath of the hipsters because I think that it has something more, that it is an affirmation of the possibility of being a whole man and I think all great literature, even contemporary literature, must have that. Then, it must have technical competence and for a young man I would say the technical competence and handling of rhythms and accents and so forth, of living speech, and in the organization of material, I would say the technical competence is great. So that all of these factors which enable us to make a contemporary judgment I think is satisfied by the book in abundance.

Mr. Bendich: Your witness, Mr. McIntosh.

CROSS-EXAMINATION BY MR. MC INTOSH

Q. How long ago did you read this book, sir?
A. I read it in manuscript.
Mr. McIntosh: That is all.

MARK LINENTHAL called as a witness on behalf of the defendant, being first duly sworn, testified as follows:

DIRECT EXAMINATION BY MR. EHRLICH

Q. Your name is Mark Linenthal?
A. That's right.
Q. And your business or occupation is?
A. I am Assistant Professor of Language Arts at San Francisco State College.
Q. How long have you been associated with San Francisco State College?
A. Three years.
Q. Have you had any other experience in matters on teaching?
A. Well, in addition to my regular work as a teacher for San Francisco State, I am also a leader of the Poetry Workshop. This is a class which is sponsored by the Poetry Department of the College. It's a class in the writing and more intelligent reading of poetry.

Q. Have you done any personal writing?

A. I have published an article in the Carolina Quarterly on the novels of Robert Van Warren. My doctoral dissertation was a critical and analytical study of the poetry and novels of Warren.

Q. Have you read People's Exhibit No. One, "Howl" by Allen Ginsberg?

A. I have.

Q. As the result of your education, your background, your teaching of this subject, your writings of articles in connection with judging in literary matters, are you able to form an opinion on the literary merit of "Howl?"

A. Yes, I am.

Q. Have you formed such an opinion?

A. I have.

Q. What is your opinion?

A. "Howl" seems to me a tremendously powerful indictment of a number of elements in the modern world, violence, greed, wastefulness, and it is cast in the form not of a moderate prose indictment, but in the form of a howl; the title of the poem seems to me metaphorical. It is as if the poet were saying, and he is saying it figuratively, the only way in which he feels in this situation it can be expressed is in language which, shall we say, exceeds the bounds of gentility.

Q. In language which howls?

A. Which is violent and powerful, which howls.

Q. After reading "Howl," I presume you gave it some thought from a technical standpoint?

A. Yes.

Q. Are you satisfied that Ginsberg in the writing of this poem sincerely and honestly sought to convey a message in his own words and after his own style?

A. I am thoroughly convinced, yes.

Mr. Ehrlich: Take the witness.

CROSS-EXAMINATION BY MR. MC INTOSH

Q. Do you know Mr. Ferlinghetti?

A. I do.

Q. How long?

A. We first met about five or six years ago.

Q. You consider him a friend of yours, is that right?

A. Yes, not an intimate friend, but a friend.

Q. Does he attend your workshop?

A. He does not.

Q. Do you attend his?

A. I do not.

Q. You haven't been over to his place hearing him read poetry is that right?

A. No I haven't.

Mr. McIntosh: All right. That's all.

Mr. Ehrlich: Step down.

Mr. Ehrlich: Mr. Blau, please.

HERBERT BLAU called as a witness on behalf of the defendant, being first duly sworn, testified as follows:

DIRECT EXAMINATION BY MR. SPEISER

Q. What is your name, address and profession?

A. Herbert Blau, 799 Clayton Street, San Francisco. I am a teacher, a writer and a theater director.

Q. Where do you teach?

A. San Francisco State College where I am an Associate Professor in the Humanities and Language Arts.

Q. And your second profession?

A. I am co-founder and consulting director of the Actors Workshop of the San Francisco Drama Guild.

Q. And the third?

A. I have written plays and critical articles for various publications, poetry, drama, modern culture.

Q. Would you name some of the publications and plays that you have authored?

A. Well, I have written a play called "Come Out of the Rain," a play called "A Gift of Fury," a number of other plays, "Prayer and Galilee"; I have written critical articles for various academic journals, Journal of Esthetic, articles of criticism, education and theater journals, New England Quarterly, some others.

Q. Have any of your plays been produced?

A. Yes, they have been produced in universities, in community theaters.

Q. Have you had an opportunity to read People's Exhibit One, "Howl and Other Poems" by Allen Ginsberg?

A. Yes, I have.

Q. Have you had an opportunity to form an opinion as to the literary merit of "Howl and Other Poems"?

A. Yes, I have.

Q. Would you give your opinion, please.

A. Yes, the thing that strikes me most forcefully about "Howl" is that it is worded in what appears to be a contemporary tradition, one that did not cause me any particular consternation in reading, a tradition, as someone previously remarked, most evident in the modern period following the first World War, a tradition that resembles European and literary tradition that is defined as "Dada," a kind of art of furious negation. By the intensity of its negation it seems to be both resurrective in quality and ultimately a sort of paean of possible hope. I wouldn't say that the chances for redemption or chances for salvation in a work of this kind are deemed to be very extensively possible, but nonetheless, the vision is not a total vision of despair. It is a vision that by the salvation of despair, by the salvation of what would appear to be perversity, by the salvation of what would appear to be illicit, is ultimately a kind of redemption of the illicit, the obscene, the disillusioned and the despairing.

Q. Would you say that the publication used language that is relevant to its purpose?

A. Well, I think most of the language of the work is designed, evidently, to be relevant to the purpose of the work, some of it succeeds; some of it doesn't. As a matter of fact, some of the language in question certainly succeeds; some of the language that has not been questioned doesn't succeed.

Q. Succeeds in accomplishing the literary purpose of the author?

A. Yes.

Mr. Speiser: I have no further questions.

CROSS-EXAMINATION BY MR. MC INTOSH

Q. Give me an example of some that doesn't succeed?

A. I think the language, apparently obscene, is language which for me almost certainly contributes to the central purpose of the work, a kind of rendition of contemporary frustration, of agonized dissent, a sort of paean of despair, a kind of condemnation. I think some of the language does not succeed, and I couldn't specify it immediately, that occasionally there is a little bit in the poem that has nothing to do with the issues in question, that the words which appear to be obscene most genuinely contribute to the sincere purpose of the work.

Q. You particularly picked those out, is that it?

A. I have picked those out only as others have. I understood I might testify today and obviously I paid some attention to language that might be held in question this afternoon.

Mr. McIntosh: That's all.

Mr. Ehrlich: All right. Mr. Foff.

ARTHUR FOFF called as a witness on behalf of the defendant, being first duly sworn, testified as follows:

DIRECT EXAMINATION BY MR. EHRLICH

Q. Your name is Arthur Foff?

A. Yes.

Q. What is your business, profession or occupation?

A. I am Associate Professor of Language Arts at San Francisco State College and a writer.

Q. You have done some writing?

A. Yes. I have done two novels, one which was put out by Lippincott and "North of Market" which is published by Harcourt, Brace, and I co-edited a text book, "Reading and Education," did part of another text book, "Introduction to the Study of Education." I did book reviewing for about seven years, for The New York Times about a year, and for the Chronicle for about seven years. I did more reviews than I care to recall and I have had stories published in a number of magazines, Kansas Review, etc.

Q. Have you had opportunity to read the prosecution's Exhibit No. One?

A. I have.

Q. As the result of your experience, your learning, your own personal writing, and the reading of Exhibit No. One, have you formed any opinion as to its literary merit?

A. I have.

Q. What is it?

A. I feel it has definite literary merit.

Mr. Ehrlich: Take the witness.

CROSS-EXAMINATION BY MR. MC INTOSH

Q. Does the City Lights Pocket Bookshop publish any of your books?

A. No, and they are not likely to.

Mr. McIntosh: That's all.

Mr. Ehrlich: Call Mr. Vincent McHugh.

VINCENT MC HUGH called as a witness on behalf of the defendant, being first duly sworn, testified as follows:

DIRECT EXAMINATION BY MR. EHRLICH

Q. Your name, address and occupation, please?

A. Vincent McHugh, 1350 Pine Street, San Francisco, I am a professional writer.

Q. How long have you been a professional writer?

A. About 40 years, I guess.

Q. Can you give us the name of some of the things you have written?

A. Yes. I have written about eight books, five novels, including "Caleb Catman's America," "Sing Before Breakfast," "I Am Thinking of My Darling," "The Victor," a book of poems called "The Blue Hen's Chickens," a text, "Primer of the Novel," a book of stories, "Edge of the World." I did about 20 years of book reviewing, mostly for the New York Evening Post, where I, for awhile, was associate editor for the literary review, The New York Times, the New York Herald Tribune, New York Sun, the Nation, and the New Republic, and for a good five years I worked on the staff of the New Yorker Mazagine as assistant to Mr. Clifton Fadiman, reviewing books and in many cases writing the lead review as a substitute for Mr. Fadiman.

Q. As the result of your training in this field, your experience, and writings, have you formed an opinion of the literary merit of People's Exhibit One, "Howl," by Allen Ginsberg?

A. Yes, sir.

Q. What is your opinion?

A. It has decided literary value and merit.

Mr. Ehrlich: Take the witness.

CROSS-EXAMINATION BY MR. MC INTOSH

Q. What is your definition of literary merit?

A. It has many definitions, but I should say that the historical body of opinion of tradition in literature as this is organized in the words of writers themselves, and the works of critics, and the whole body of literature, and carried down to us who inherit it today, that, I think constitutes the ground for judging literary merit, and that it have value and force of tradition, gives us some means to determine even a brand new work that just came out of somebody's hands yesterday. In this case, for example, we have a vision of a modern hell. Now, we have certain precedents for that, for example, Pound's cantos, especially Cantos Fourteen and Fifteen. These, for example, in turn derive certainly from Dante and Dante, in turn, derives from the Odyssey, and so on into all the mythologies of the World. I think we do have a certain body of opinion, certain grounds for establishing literary merit.

Mr. McIntosh: That's all.

Mr. Ehrlich: Step down, sir. It now gives me great pleasure to inform the court that the defense rests.

Pardon me, your Honor. My attention has been called to this mass of book reviews. Your Honor did say that you thought these matters should be brought to the court's attention.

Mr. McIntosh: Now, just a moment.

The Court: No, I didn't say I thought that they should be brought to the Court's attention. I mentioned book reviews along with my suggestions for an outline of the testimony which might be produced if the parties so decided. I make my position clear again that I have not requested nor asked for the production of any testimony. Whatever testimony is introduced is done at the option of the respective parties and not at my request.

Mr. Ehrlich: Well, I didn't mean to put it that way, your Honor, but reference has been made to reviews throughout the country by both the prosecution and the defense. I therefore offer in evidence these photostats of reviews to be marked as one exhibit. They are from The New York Times Book Review and by William Hogan in the San Francisco Chronicle.

Mr. McIntosh: I will object to any offer—

The Court: Wait a minute. Let counsel finish.

Mr. McIntosh: That is one way of getting before his Honor things which are not permissible.

The Court: Let Mr. Ehrlich finish his offer and then I will listen to your objection.

Mr. Ehrlich: Then there is a list of Winter Books in which there is a review of the book in question, one from the Nation, a photostat, your Honor, of its book review, and The New York Times Book Review in its own printing. I offer these as one exhibit merely for the purpose of informing the Court of the opinion of reviewers concerning the literary merit of Howl.

The Court: Are these reviews all pertaining to "Howl?"

Mr. Ehrlich: All pertain to "Howl."

The Court: And are they prior to the commencement of this action?

Mr. Ehrlich: Oh, yes, February 21st—

The Court: Well, you don't have to go over the dates, but they are all prior to the commencement of this action?

Mr. Ehrlich: Every one in this group, yes.

The Court: Now, I will listen to your objection, Mr. McIntosh.

Mr. McIntosh: I object to them as being incompetent, irrelevant and immaterial, no foundation for the production of them before your Honor. The only possible reason that he could offer those would be if there was some testimony by Mr. Ferlinghetti; if he were to take the stand and say that he relied upon those book reviews in selling this book. There is no testimony to that effect. That only goes to the intent, your Honor.

The Court: What only goes to the intent?

Mr. McIntosh: If that were true, if Mr. Ferlinghetti took the stand and said that he relied upon these book reviews in selling the book and that he didn't know there was anything obscene in there, under the cases we have here in California.

The Court: The Wepplo case?

Mr. McIntosh: Yes, I think there is dicta in there to that effect. That would be the only possible way Mr. Ehrlich could introduce that type of evidence.

The Court: People versus Creative Age Press, 79 New York Supplement Second 198: Over counsel's objection a collection of clippings was introduced in evidence taken from a considerable number of newspapers and periodicals of general circulation containing reviews by literary critics and the case states: "The practice of referring to such reviews in cases of this nature has become well established." And it cites Halsey versus New York Society for the Suppression of Vice, United States versus Ulysses, People versus Gotham Book Mart, and then going further: "Opinions of professional critics publicly disseminated in the ordinary course of their employment are proper aids to the Court in weighing the author's sincerity of purpose and the literary worth of his effort. These are factors which, while not determining whether a book is obscene, are to be considered in deciding that question. Such expressions of opinion can be of aid to the Court only to the extent that it determines it may rely on

them as disinterested and well founded. That is why I asked
if they had been published prior to the instigation of this
case. So, your objection will be overruled on the basis of that
authority—

Mr. McIntosh: What state is that out of, Judge?

The Court: That is New York. And California has so far
adopted a more liberal attitude than the State of New York,
which has in turn a fairly liberal attitude on this subject. The
offer is accepted.

Mr. Ehrlich: As one exhibit, your Honor?

The Court: As one exhibit, and I was going to ask Mr.
McIntosh whether he wanted an opportunity to present any
testimony in rebuttal.

Mr. McIntosh: Yes, your Honor.

The Court: All right. I would suggest this, then, anticipating your question Mr. Ehrlich. We allow Mr. McIntosh to
present any rebuttal testimony that he may have and at the
conclusion of that rebuttal testimony, if the defense desires
not to submit any additional testimony at that time, both of
you should be prepared to argue the matter and to submit
any authorities that you have in writing.

Mr. Ehrlich: Your Honor will bear in mind that we didn't
know what the rebuttal testimony is going to be. I don't want
to be required to go ahead with argument and submission if
any issue is raised by the prosecution that has not been raised
up to now.

The Court: That's unless something does take you by sur-
prise, which I very much doubt. Mr. McIntosh, do you have
any rebuttal?

Mr. McIntosh: Yes, your Honor.

The Court: All right.

DAVID KIRK called as a witness on behalf of the people, being
first duly sworn, testified as follows:

DIRECT EXAMINITION BY MR. MC INTOSH

Q. Will you state your name, sir?

A. David Kirk.

Q. And where do you live?

A. 1021 Menlo Oaks Drive, Menlo Park.

Q. What is your business or occupation at the present?

A. I am an Assistant Professor of English at the University of San Francisco.

Q. How long have you been so employed?

A. I am in my eighth year.

Q. And previous to that time did you have some connection with Stanford?

A. I was an assistant instructor at Stanford, yes.

Q. For how long?

A. About two and a half years.

Q. And are you presently taking some work there at Stanford?

A. Yes, I'm finishing my Ph.D. degree at Stanford.

Q. And have you also written, published poetry at times?

A. On occasion in the past I have published some poetry, yes.

Q. Now, at my request you have looked at People's No. One in Evidence, the edition called "Howl and Other Poems" by Allen Ginsberg?

A. I have.

Q. And have you formed an opinion, sir, as to whether or not that publication has any literary value?

A. I formed an opinion. It's my opinion that if it has any literary value, it is negligible.

Q. Negligible. Can you explain that to us, Mr. Kirk, how you arrived at that opinion?

A. There are many bases for criticism, of course, subjective and objective. I endeavored to arrive at my opinion on an objective basis. For example, a great literary work, or even fairly great literary work, would obviously be exceedingly successful in form, but this poem is really just a weak imitation of a form that was used 80 to 90 years ago by Walt Whitman, imitation.

Q. Do you recall the title of that poem?

A. "Leaves of Grass" would be the name of the poem. Literary value could also reside in theme, and what little literary value there is in "Howl" it seems to me does come in theme. The statement of the idea of the poem was relatively clear, but it has little validity, and, therefore, the theme has a negative value, no value at all.

The third basis of objective criticism would be the—well, what for lack of a better term, I would call opportunity. The poet or the writer and his time and his problems—pardon me —the problems of the time, should have some kind of significant interaction. This poem is apparently dedicated to a long-dead movement—"Dadaism"—and some late followers of Dadaism. And, therefore, the opportunity is long past for any significant literary contribution of this poem. Those are my objective bases.

Mr. McIntosh: All right. You may cross-examine.

CROSS-EXAMINATION BY MR. EHRLICH

Q. You have done some writing?

A. In a small way, yes.

Q. And you have done some studying of literature generally, I take it?

A. Yes, the last ten years of my life have been spent in that.

Q. In what field did you do this studying?

A. My specialty is the English Novel. I have concentrated, however, on all English Literature from 1660 to date, and do teach courses in such works.

Q. What subject did you instruct?

A. Well, I taught freshman English and Engineering English and narration during that period.

Q. You set out three bases which you used as guides in your evaluation of poetic works, is that right?

A. Yes, my objective bases.

Q. Do you apply those three guides to your evaluation of every poetic work?

A. Yes, that is my consistent objective aim.

Q. Have you had occasion to review poetry for the general public?

A. Oh, for publication, no.

Q. These three guides which you have set up, do you use them in instructing your classes?

A. That is correct.

Q. Are your three guides accepted by men who are critics of poetry? Are they accepted as rules to be followed or are those just your bases?"

A. Doubtless they are accepted by some critics of poetry because they are fairly standard rules.

Q. I see. Some accept it and some do not.

A. That's right. There is another general basis, the subjective basis of criticism. They would not accept such bases.

Q. Did I understand you to say that Ginsberg used the Walt Whitman style?

A. The form, the form of the book, "Leaves of Grass."

Q. That Ginsberg used the same format or form—is that what you are saying?

A. That's right.

Q. And because of Ginsberg's using that format, it is your opinion that the poem "Howl" has no literary value or merit, is that right?

A. On the basis of form, that is correct, because great literature always creates its own form for each significant occasion.

Q. By that you do not mean that Walt Whitman's "Leaves of Grass" doesn't quite qualify?

A. That is great literature; the form was created by Walt Whitman.

Q. And it is great literature?

A. Right.

Q. And that form is a great form?

A. That's right.

Q. All right.

A. For Walt Whitman and on that occasion.

Q. And at the same time you say that because Ginsberg copied that format, "Howl" has no value or merit, is that correct, sir?

A. That is correct. An imitation never does have the value of the original.

Q. Have you ever imitated anything, Mr. Kirk?

A. In forming what little style I have, of course I have. Every student in trying to form his own style obviously begins on a basis of imitation, not of just one writer, but of many writers.

Q. Well, then, in your opinion, Mr. Kirk, it is good to imitate, isn't it?

A. As a student exercise, yes, but it does not create literature.

Q. Who did Walt Whitman copy?

A. To my knowledge, no one.

Q. You don't know, isn't that your answer, you don't know?

A. That's right.

Q. I understand your next sign post to be that the idea of "Howl" is clear, but has little validity. Do I quote you correctly?

A. That is the general conclusion, yes, in theme; the idea of "Howl" is clear in theme.

Q. In theme. Well now, you'll have to explain that a little bit to me, if you will. The idea is good, we agree on that, do we?

A. No, we do not. The idea is clear.

Q. The idea is clear. I didn't understand you. Now, what is the idea of Ginsberg in "Howl?" What idea does he have there?

A. Well, he celebrates the unfortunate life of—I can't remember the man's name—Solomon—the unfortunate life of the man, Solomon, who is a drifter of dadaist persuasion.

Q. Drift what?

A. Drifter of dadaist persuasion.

Q. He portrays that?

A. That's correct.

Q. And does that portrayal have any validity?

A. Not as literature, no.

Q. Now, let's take one step at a time. Is there any validity as he is telling the story as he sees it?

A. A representation of Solomon's life. I take it on faith that it must be a valid, true picture.

Q. And then when Ginsberg goes a little bit further and he condemns this existence, which has soured and engulfed Solomon, that is a valid description of what Ginsberg feels, is that right, sir?

A. I am sorry, but I didn't identify any condemnation.

Q. You didn't?

A. No, I found only sympathy.

Q. Well, let's put it your way. This sympathy which Ginsberg shows for Solomon, would you say that that is honestly portrayed as Ginsberg saw it?

A. As an individual writer, yes.

Q. What impression do you have of the end of the third portion of "Howl"? What is your understanding of it?

A. My understanding there would be based on a reference to the value, the value statement of the third portion, wherein the poet expresses the usual dadaist line that everything is created for man's despair and everything must be forgotten and destroyed, and that Solomon's life apparently has had this kind of rhythm. Therefore, there is some validity of theme, you see, in that area.

Q. Then there is validity of theme there?

A. As a dadaist statement, yes.

Q. Well, I don't care what qualifications you put on it, but there is some validity to Ginsberg's theme, isn't there, whether you personally approve of it, or not?

A. Well, I am afraid that I have got my tongue tripped up here—this clarity—I should have said "clarity" instead of "validity."

Q. But you have been using the term validity all of the time you have been on the stand. By the way, Mr. Kirk, have you read the Holy Bible?

A. I have.

Q. You and I don't know who wrote Job, do we?

A. I am sure I didn't.

Q. Or do you know?

Mr. McIntosh: I will object to that, your Honor. He is going far afield.

The Court: What is the purpose of the question?

Mr. Ehrlich: The witness testified that Ginsberg said everything was created for the destruction of man. I want to make some comparisons to ascertain whether the witness knows the subject or whether he is just testifying. If he has read Job, as he says he has, let's compare it. This man is an expert.

The Court: He's testified as to three bases or to three premises on which he made a determination.

Mr. Ehrlich: Yes, but he said in answering one of my questions that the third portion of "Howl" merely is a condemnation of the world as it treated man exemplified by Solomon. Is that correct, sir?

A. The third portion of the book is that area in which the dadaist theme of the unworthiness of life, of the necessity of forgetting all past history, of the necessity for starting over life again and wiping out everything in the past is celebrated.

Q. Now tell me, did you read Job?

A. I have.

Q. Isn't Job crying the very same cry as Ginsberg's "Howl"?

A. Not at all . . .

Mr. McIntosh: I object and ask the answer be stricken, your Honor.

The Court: Motion granted.

Mr. Ehrlich: Q. Well, isn't it a fact that other writers have condemned life and its application to mankind as well as Ginsberg?

A. I suppose. I don't know of any individual example at this moment.

Q. May I suggest Job to you, Mr. Kirk?

A. Yes.

Q. And would you agree with me, sir, that Job does condemn life?

A. Not to the same end that the Dadaist does, no.

Q. Well, let's leave the Dadaist out. Let's just stick with Job and "Howl" for a moment. Doesn't Job condemn the position of man's fortune on earth?

Mr. McIntosh: I will object to any comparison with the Bible, your Honor, as to what Job said.

The Court: No. The witness stated that he didn't know of any particular example of any writer in the same vein and he stated that he has read Job and that Job, I presume, counsel is going to show that Job does cover the same theme in somewhat the same way. I don't know whether—

Mr. Ehrlich: That is right.

The Court: I think that is what he is driving at. So I will overrule the objection. Mr. Kirk, so that you won't be confused that requires a "yes" or "no" answer, and you may explain your answer after you have answered it. In other words, you are not confined to a "yes" or a "no" answer.

The Witness: Job does condemn man's condition, then,

yes, but he does not go on then as the Dadaist goes on to desire to wipe out all memory of the past, to wipe out all human memory of everything that the human race has ever done so that there can be a fresh start made as the Dadaist does.

Mr. Ehrlich: Q. And that's one of the reasons why you think "Howl" has no validity, because it wants to wipe out everything and start over, is that it?

A. Well, no. That was the only small validity that I found in "Howl" because that gives it some literary merit, some message of some sort.

Q. Mr. Kirk, I am quoting from the Holy Bible and I must assume that these are the words of Job:

"When shall I arrive, and the night begone? And I am full of tossings to and fro unto the dawning of the day.

"My flesh is clothed with worms and clods of dust; my skin is broken, and become loathsome.

"My days are swifter than a weaver's shuttle, and are spent without hope.

"Therefore I will not refrain my mouth; I will speak in the anguish of my spirit; I will complain in the bitterness of my soul.

"When I say, my bed shall not comfort me, my couch shall ease my complaint;

"Then thou scarest me with dreams, and terrifiest me through visions:

"So that my soul chooseth strangling, and death rather than my life.

"I loathe it; I would not live always, let me alone; for my days are vanity.

"I have sinned; what shall I do unto thee, O thou preserver of man? Why hast thou set me as a mark against thee, so that I am a burden to myself?

"And why dost thou not pardon my transgression, and take away my iniquity? For now shall I sleep in the dust; and thou shalt seek me in the morning, but I shall not be."

Q. In theme, where is Job different from Ginsberg's third portion of "Howl"?

A. There seems no resemblance at all, just a vast difference.

Q. In your mind there is no resemblance, but I am talking about the words.

A. In the words, there is no resemblance.

Q. None?

A. No resemblance, neither in style nor in theme nor in opportunity.

Q. In other words, you think, Mr. Kirk, that all thinking of all men must go through the same funnel, is that it?

A. I do not understand.

Q. Isn't Job condemning the futility of life as Ginsberg condemns the futility of life?

A. Not at all. Job may be condemning the suffering of his own life, futility of his own life, but he is not condemning anything that's being talked about in "Howl."

Q. Well, what is Ginsberg doing with Solomon? Isn't he doing the same thing only speaking in the third person?

A. I found no air of condemnation in the poem at all.

The Court: I think the word you used was "sympathy," wasn't it?

The Witness: I did find sympathy, yes.

Mr. Ehrlich: Q. Are you teaching poetry now?

A. Yes.

Q. Where?

A. At the University of San Francisco.

Q. Isn't Job the same type of condemnation that Ginsberg seeks to make in "Howl"?

A. I—

The Court: Pardon me, Mr. Kirk. May I interrupt you, Mr. Ehrlich? You are going to be at cross-purposes here because the witness has several times stated that "Howl" is not condemnation. Am I correct in that?

The Witness: Yes.

The Court: So that you are using a word there that has not been used by this witness. In other words, your premise is wrong as a basis of the question.

Mr. Ehrlich: Yes, your Honor. Either this testimony means that Ginsberg has condemned life or that Ginsberg has not condemned life. He said a few moments ago, as I understood it, that Ginsberg was preaching the futility of all life, that we ought to wipe it all out and apparently start all over.

Q. Did I understand that correctly, sir?

A. That's not clearly stated in the poem, but he identifies sympathy with the Dadaist theme, he identifies his sympathy with their aim, that is, the Dadaist aim.

Q. And what is the Dadaist aim? Let's get that into the record?

A. Well, as a literary movement about 1918 to 1921, this group of French writers decided that the world was in such a mess that the only hope for the world was to destroy all memory of everything that men had ever accomplished through history, that each individual should destroy all memory of everything that ever happened to him, that language and communications should be destroyed, and then on that basis perhaps a fresh start toward a better world might be made. That is a generalization of the Dadaist theme.

Q. In your opinion, that is what Ginsberg has tried to do, is that right, sir?

A. As he portrays the life of Solomon, who is identified as a Dadaist, and shows sympathy with Solomon, who is identified as a Dadaist, he seems to indicate that he has a friendship toward that idea, yes.

Q. And you don't believe in that philosophy, do you?

A. Not at all. It has been dead since about 1922 or '23 when the followers moved into the area of surrealism almost unanimously.

Q. That does not necessarily mean that a person who does think that is wrong, does it?

A. No, but that does not create literature.

Q. Well, what creates literature, Mr. Kirk?

A. I'd have to return to my three bases for an objective criticism.

Q. Those are three you gave?

A. Form, theme and opportunity.

Q. Well, let's get to the third one, then. Your third point is opportunity, sir?

A. That is correct.

Q. And when you say "opportunity" you mean what, with relation to the subject matter here?

A. Well, as I first said, the word "opportunity" I inserted for the want of a better word. It means the correlation of the poet and his ideas with his time and with all times. Great pieces of literature appear with a definite message and application to the problems of the particular time in which they appear, and if they are great pieces of literature they continue to have this validity and they continue to have a message. There is opportunity.

Q. Well, do you think that Ginsberg, in his travels had the opportunity to observe life and to write about it?

A. A small segment, yes.

Q. And this is the segment he is writing about, is that not true?

A. One thing—

Q. Answer that, sir "yes" or "no," please.

A. I am confused.

Q. This is the segment he is writing about, isn't that right, sir?

A. I can't answer that either "Yes" or "No."

Q. You say that in his travels he wrote about a small segment of the community.

A. Here is where the confusion comes in: I believe the travels are Solomon's, isn't that right?

Q. What is that, please?

A. I believe the travels are Solomon's, not Ginsberg's. That is the basis of my confusion.

Q. Well, Ginsberg is writing it about Solomon; it's his own observations. You have read that, haven't you?

A. Yes.

Q. All right. You know Ginsberg wrote about it, don't you?

A. Know that he wrote the poem, yes.

Q. And you know in Solomon he is depicting his own travels?

A. No, I do not know that.

Q. All right. He is depicting the travels of someone else?

A. That seems to me—

Q. And watches them? He's watching the travels of this man Solomon and he is describing them, isn't that right?

A. That is what appears to be there, yes.

Q. Yes. Now, he had the opportunity to do so, isn't that right?

A. What is the antecedent to "he"?

Q. Ginsberg.

A. Ginsberg—I don't know.

Q. Then, not knowing, you are unable to form an opinion as to whether he did or did not have the opportunity to write this?

A. I am unable to know whether he has an acquaintance with Solomon. That is the thing beyond my experience, beyond my knowledge.

Q. Well, let me ask you Mr. Kirk, whether you know Ginsberg or Solomon or whether Ginsberg knew Solomon or not,—we're talking about this work and about the impression you get of this work, and your answer now is that you don't know whether Ginsberg knows Solomon.

A. That is correct.

Q. Do you evaluate a work by knowing whether the writer knew the person he is talking about?

A. Absolutely.

Q. In "Vanity Fair" was Becky Sharp a personal friend of the author?

A. I don't think so, no.

Q. Well, would you say that "Vanity Fair" is one of the great outstanding works of literature?

A. That is correct.

Q. And you don't know—

A. I am certain Becky Sharp never lived as an individual, if that's what you are driving at.

Q. Are you certain that Solomon lived?

A. No.

Q. Then you don't know, do you?

A. Not at all.

Q. So that your former answer that you couldn't answer my question as to whether Ginsberg was properly describing Solomon's life is that you do not know whether Ginsberg knew Solomon and therefore you couldn't tell whether he was properly describing it?

A. I didn't say that I did not know Solomon; I said that I did not know if he knew Solomon.

Q. Let's go back to Becky Sharp and "Vanity Fair." Did Becky Sharp know the author?

A. That is a frivolous question.

Q. Is that a frivolous question?

A. Yes.

Mr. McIntosh: Already asked and answered, too.

Mr. Ehrlich: The answer, I think, to every question is frivolous when he can't answer it.

Mr. McIntosh: I will object to these scurrilous remarks.

Mr. Ehrlich: If it is scurrilous it's not intended to be offensive to Mr. Kirk, but he can't answer the question.

The Court: All right, gentlemen. Next question.

Mr. Ehrlich: Q. Well, a lot of books have been written over the years depicting life as the writer saw it. That's generally true, isn't it, sir?

A. I am under that impression.

Q. Yes. Now, you have heard of Erasmus, haven't you?

A. I have.

Q. And Erasmus was quite a writer, wasn't he?

A. I have little acquaintance with Erasmus. My study begins with 1660.

Q. 1660. You wouldn't dare go back a day before 1660, would you?

Mr. McIntosh: Object to that, your Honor.

The Court: The objection is sustained. Mr. Ehrlich, the witness is entitled to courtesy on the stand. The Court admonishes you to treat him with courtesy and refrain from badgering the witness.

Mr. Ehrlich: Q. Well, let me tell you about Erasmus, then. Maybe you did read about it and have forgotten it. He wrote a great deal—

Mr. McIntosh: I'll object to that type of question, your Honor, telling him a story and then going to ask him a question on it.

Mr. Ehrlich: Let me tell him about Erasmus. He doesn't know anything about Erasmus, just heard about it. As I understand, he wasn't completely acquainted with—

The Court: Let me hear the question.

Mr. Ehrlich: Q. Eramus did a great deal of writing, and one of the things he wrote which has come down to us through the years is a little work titled "In Praise of Folly." Do you recall ever reading that?

A. I have never read it.

Q. Well, have you read Voltaire?

A. I read one work, "Candide."

Q. What is your opinion of "Candide?"

A. As literature? It is great literature.

Q. When you say "great literature," you mean what?

A. I'd have to return to the three bases again for objective criticism, form, theme, opportunity.

Q. He copied Walt Whitman's style, is that right?

A. Not Voltaire, no.

Q. Whose style did Voltaire copy?

A. I do not know enough about French stylists and French forms to answer that. I have read the work only in translation.

Q. So there is some qualification to style copying to which you originally referred?

A. I don't see there is. No.

Mr. McIntosh: Oh—

Mr. Ehrlich: Please.

The Court: Well, Counsel has a right to make an objection.

Mr. Ehrlich: If he objects.

Mr. McIntosh: I would like to. I didn't want to box with him, he's disturbing me. I get my mouth open and out fly fists.

Mr. Ehrlich: Q. Well now, going back to Voltaire, and the only thing you read written by Voltaire—by the way, you know how much he wrote, don't you?

A. I have a general idea.

Q. Safe to say that he wrote hundreds and hundreds of things, didn't he?

A. Without a doubt.

Q. Now, getting back to "Candide," would you say that Voltaire had the idea of "Candide" as a clearcut idea?

A. That's not my recollection of it, no. It took some little reflection to get at an approximation of the idea.

Q. Well, did you feel that there was any validity in the nature and character of his work?

A. That's the memory I have of "Candide," yes.

Q. Well, if you had difficulty in understanding what Voltaire's idea was, how can you come to the conclusion—or give us your reason for coming to the conclusion that it had validity?

A. Upon the basis of reflection.

Q. What was your reflection?

A. Well, I am afraid it's been 10 or 12 years since I read this. The pattern of reflection would be difficult to recall. My identification as a valid theme would not come immediately upon reading "Candide," only upon reflection.

Q. How long have you reflected on "Howl?"

A. Let's see. What is the date?

The Court: Today is the 19th of September.

The Witness: 19th. I believe two weeks.

Mr. Ehrlich: Q. Two weeks?

A. Two weeks would be the limit of my opportunity, however, I made up my mind after five minutes.

Q. Two weeks was the limit of your opportunity. And you reflected for a long, long time on Voltaire's "Candide," is that right?

A. Exactly. A great work of literature frequently conveys all kinds of challenges.

Q. Well, do you believe that if you reflected for another ten years on "Howl" that you might change your opinion?

A. I am quite certain I would not.

Q. You are quite certain today that you will not change your mind in the next ten years, is that right, sir?

A. That is correct.

Mr. Ehrlich: That is all.

GAIL POTTER called as a witness on behalf of the people, being first duly sworn, testified as follows:

DIRECT EXAMINATION BY MR. MC INTOSH

Q. May I have your name, please?

A. Gail Potter.

Q. And where do you reside?

A. 21 Bella Vista Way, San Francisco.

Q. I see. And what is your occupation?

A. My occupation is teaching.

Q. I see. Now, I believe you have a degree from Stanford, is that right?

A. I have a degree from Stanford. The fact is I have attended nine universities in Europe and America.

Q. Will you list them and tell us what degrees you have in some way, if you can remember them all?

A. Would you like to know—some of the places I didn't work for degrees.

Q. I see.

A. I was at State Normal School, I graduated from a professional school of music and drama, two years, graduated from the State University of Nebraska, I graduated from Stanford, I went to school at Wisconsin University, New York University, University of Southern California, London University, and in Salzberg, Austria.

Q. I see. Now, you made advanced studies at a lot of these universities?

A. Some of them were advanced studies.

Q. I see. And have you done any writing yourself?

A. Yes, I have done considerable. I was on an NBC station ten years while I was teaching, Community Service Director, and I was Educational Coordinator; I have rewritten "Faust" —took three years to do that, but I did it; I rewrote "Everyman."

Now, that isn't as funny as you might think.

The Court: Pardon me, Madam. Ladies and gentlemen, we are not playing games; this is a trial that involves serious issues. Now kindly accord the witness the courtesy that you would want to be accorded. I know occasionally you can't help this laughter, but please try to maintain decorum in the courtroom; otherwise, I will have to clear it.

The Witness: May I say something else about that?

The Court: You just answer the questions of the District Attorney. He will ask you if he wants any more information.

The Witness: All right.

Mr. McIntosh: Q. Well, I think you wanted to tell us about some of the books you have rewritten?

A. Forty Fausts—I wrote from the Forty Fausts, so it isn't laughable unless you have read only one, which most of you probably have—excuse me. Then I also have written thirty-five feature articles for the last two or three years, and all of the time I was on this radio station I wrote "Drama in the News" once a week in cooperation with Time Magazine, Life Magazine sent galley proofs to criticize, and also I had Romance and Music Series, taking the great musicians and writing dramas on their lives, and I was on the station ten years besides my university work; I wrote "Know Your City," the series of articles for one city, for which I was paid, of course, and then I wrote a pageant for one of the big affairs in Florida.

Q. Now, you have done some teaching, also?

A. I have taught 15 years in universities.

Q. Various colleges, is that right?

A. Yes, at three different colleges.

Q. Which ones?

A. I taught at Golden Gate College when it was a city college—I taught there for three years; Dominican College, two years; and the College of Southern Florida for ten years.

Q. I see. Now then, at my request did you have an opportunity to take a look at "Howl," People's No. One in evidence?

A. Yes, I did; I have had the opportunity.

Q. All right. And did you form an opinion as to whether or not the book called "Howl and Other Poems" has any literary merit?

A. I think it has no literary merit.

Q. Go ahead.

A. I think you cannot separate literary style and literary content.

Q. I see. Now, could you give us some idea of how you arrived at your opinion?

A. To have literary style you must have form, diction, fluidity, clarity. Now, I am speaking only of style, and in content, every great piece of literature, anything that can really be classified as literature of some moral greatness, and I think this fails to the nth degree.

Q. I see. Can you think of any other reasons?

A. Yes, use of language. Now, in regard to the figures of speech which he uses, he fails in rhetoric, of course, for one thing, because his figures of speech are crude and you feel like you are going through the gutter when you have to read that stuff. I didn't linger on it too long, I assure you.

Mr. McIntosh: You may cross-examine.

Mr. Ehrlich: Step down.

The Witness: There is something else you want?

Mr. Ehrlich: Step down.

Mr. McIntosh: Mr. Ehrlich doesn't want to cross-examine.

The Witness: Are you through with me?

Mr. Ehrlich: Step down.

The Witness: Oh, thank you; thank you, Mr. Ehrlich.

Mr. Ehrlich: Thank you, Miss Potter.

Mr. McIntoch: The People rest, your Honor.

The Court: Any surrebuttal?

Mr. Ehrlich: None, your Honor.

The Court: All right. Both sides have rested. I will hear from the prosecution.

Mr. McIntosh: All right, your Honor.

We only brought two rebuttal witnesses here today merely for the purpose of showing that sometimes the experts do not agree. Now, you know very well throughout this trial I have taken the position that the opinion of experts as to literary merit of this particular book, "Howl" is irrelevant. However, the Court has allowed experts to testify and I believe for the purpose of aiding your Honor in coming to a proper decision. However, I would like to point this out: Our courts, of course, have held that certain types of books, for example, medical books, even though they may contain words which may be obscene by themselves, if they are proper to the text, illustrating something in the medical books, that they are not obscene; the books are not obscene per se. In other words, they are written for the medical profession alone, and as long as they were written for the medical profession, if they are not written for the general public, why, then, the courts have generally agreed that they are not in the purview of obscenity statutes of practically all the states.

Now, here we have a book, "Howl," contains words, if by themselves, that is, taken just by themselves, your Honor, I believe they are words, are definitely obscene. And we have had different literary experts testify that the books have literary merit, that the words are necessary to that so-called merit. I believe Mark Schorer testified to that effect, and some of the others, and even Mark Schorer, stated that the book necessarily must use a language of vulgarity, that is to say, to illustrate the theme of "Howl." But it's funny in our law; we are allowed to use expert witnesses to testify as to literary merit, but we are not allowed to bring in, we will say, the average man to testify that when he read the book he doesn't understand it, doesn't know what it's all about; perhaps it's over his head.

But is that book written for him, your Honor, the average man, or is it written for the literary expert, or I would say the expert on modern poetry; that is what the book has been termed, I believe, by defense witnesses, particularly Mark Schorer? Is this book pointed for that particular type of person, those who understand modern poetry in what they call the San Francisco Renaissance? Well, certainly a book, your

Honor, is written to be sold on the stands to the average person, the general person who is here to buy it, not just particularly pointed to the literary expert, because it's not like a medical book written for them alone; it's written for a person who walks in to buy it. And I think that when the book is written it should be considered as its effect upon the average person who is going to buy it, not the modern person.

Now, for example, Mark Schorer—I believe he was the one who said something about surrealistic paintings. He likened "Howl" to such things. Now, surrealistic paintings, I believe, were mentioned even by Mr. Kirk, of the Modern School, and you have seen these paintings at various museums; I know you have. And we have seen them, splotches of paint going this way, circular lines going this way, diagonals and all this sort of thing. And modern painters have described what they mean in knowing terms, sometimes a lot of double-talk about it, but, anyway, they have described them as having some meaning. Sometimes they have been rather red-faced to find out that some of their prize winners have turned out to be the work, for example, one case of a monkey doing finger-painting. In another case, where a boy threw a paint brush at a canvas, a big splotch, and they entered that in a modern painting exhibition and it won a prize.

Well, there is the modern, surrealistic painter, the modern person, the person who reads modern poetry, who understands that. I don't believe the average citizen understands surrealistic paintings, nor does he understand modern painting or poetry. Take "Howl," for example: I have read it; I can't put on witnesses to testify that they have read it and don't know what it's all about. Frankly—I made the comment in open court here that I read it; I don't understand it very well. In fact, looking it all over, I think it is a lot of sensitive bullshit, using the language of Mr. Ginsberg. So then, if the sale of a book is not being limited to just the modern book reviewers and experts on modern poetry, but falls into the hands of the general public, that is, the average reader, this court should take that into consideration in determining whether or not "Howl" is obscene under Section 311.

The test as outlined in the Roth case—I would like to read that again, your Honor, because I think it shows the position of what you will have to do in deciding this case, to take the position of the average reader. I would like to read that again, your Honor, if I may. In the Roth case, on page 1509, going down a little ways, it says that:

"The test is not whether it would arouse sexual desires or sexual impure thoughts in those comprising a particular segment of the community, the young, the immature, or the highly prudish or would leave another segment, the scientific or highly educated or the so-called worldly-wise and sophisticated indifferent and unmoved.

"The test in each case is the effect of the book, picture or publication considered as a whole, not upon any particular class, but upon all those whom it is likely to reach. In other words, you determine its impact upon the average person in the community. The books, pictures and circulars must be judged as a whole, in their entire context, and you are not to consider detached or separate portions in reaching a conclusion. You judge the circulars, pictures and publications which have been put in evidence by present-day standards of the community. You may ask yourself does it offend the common conscience of the community by present-day standards.

"In this case, ladies and gentlemen of the jury, you and you alone are the exclusive judges of what the common conscience of the community is, and in determining that conscience, you are to consider the community as a whole, young and old, educated and uneducated, the religious and the irreligious—men, women and children."

Now, I think that sums up pretty well what the average man is, the average person that's going to buy this book, and it is not published just for the modern reader of poetry who understands modern poetry. I think that should be taken into consideration.

Now then, I believe your Honor has no quarrel with the statement in Wepplo, and also in some of the cases cited therein, to the effect that the fact that a book has literary merit does not prevent it from being obscene if otherwise it has that character. I don't believe you have any quarrel with that.

Now, let's look at the obscene character of the book. I'm not going to repeat to you or read any of the passages; we have had enough of that here, I believe, to present you with the obscene words. But in determining the obscenity of this book, your Honor, I would like to ask you this: Does the fact that poetry is bound in a book give it any immunity from an obscenity statute? because Section 311 certainly covers writings, papers, books, pictures, or prints. The mere fact it is bound in a volume doesn't give it any immunity whatsoever. And going back to some of this other modern poetry such as surrealism, would the picture, for example, of genitals under the guise of surrealistic painting give the painting immunity just by itself?

The Court: Well, aren't you being a little impractical there? In your surrealistic paintings you can't readily recognize any object.

Mr. McIntosh: I grant you that. That is what I am talking about.

The Court: So you couldn't recognize genitals; they wouldn't be portrayed as such.

Mr. McIntosh: In one of these books here—I don't know whether they have it here. No, they don't have all the dirty books. I can't think of the name of it now but anyway in one of the works there are pictures of various things which are very violently done, but anybody can see what they are talking about and see what they are portraying. That's what I'm getting at, your Honor. I will go along with you; I can look at one of those modern paintings and I can't tell what it's all about myself. I would like you to ask yourself, your Honor, in determining whether or not these books are obscene, would you like to see this sort of poetry printed in your local newspaper, that is to say, to be read by your family, that type of thing? or would you like to have this poetry read to you over the air on the radio as a diet? In other words, your Honor, how far are we going to license the use of filthy, vulgar, obscene and disgusting language? How far can we go? And I might say, you might note that the newspapers, the television, the radio, they don't use that type of words at all. Do you know the reason? Because that consumption is for the average reader. That's the one we are trying to protect here.

The Court: I would like to put a question to you, Mr. McIntosh. Can you point to—or rather, will you point to any particular part, passage or parts of "Howl" which you contend arouse prurient interest?

Mr. McIntosh: I don't know how far you can go with a word like "fuck," your Honor.

The Court: Perhaps we don't understand one another. The mere use of that word, you might say as a cussword or as an epithet, would not necessarily arouse prurient interest. In other words, you may use coarse or vulgar words, so-called coarse or vulgar words, without arousing prurient interest. Now, the cases all hold that regardless of whether there are coarse or vulgar epithets, they must be such as to arouse a prurient interest according to Mr. Justice Brennan in the latest Supreme Court decision. So for the court's guidance, and for something that the defense should meet, I wish that you would call to my attention what parts you feel would tend to arouse impure thoughts, impure sexual thoughts or prurient interest.

Mr. McIntosh: I think, your Honor, perhaps you are confining me to one issue of what the definition of obscenity is. If you would look in Corpus Juris.

The Court: Don't cite Corpus Juris. That is mere text-book language. The test of obscenity, while it is never certain and can never be definite and varies from community to community and from the changing times, has at least been given some interpretation by the courts of this state, the courts of New York State, the courts of Massachusetts, the courts of Pennsylvania, and finally in the Roth case by the United States Supreme Court. Now, if I recall correctly, all of those cases state that the use of coarse or vulgar words, in the absence of their arousing prurient interests, is not obscenity.

Mr. McIntosh: Well, we have Gore versus State, 545 Southeastern 2nd 79, Georgia Appellate, it states this: "The word 'obscene,' as used in the statute making possession or exhibition of obscene pictures, etc., a felony, means not only language suggestive of sexual intercourse or tending to excite lewdness or to debauch the public morals, but means offensive to the senses, repulsive, disgusting, foul, filthy, offensive to modesty."

The Court: That is not the rule today, but just for the sake of argument, assuming that my premise is correct, without conceding anything on your part, can you point to any parts of "Howl" that you feel would excite prurient interest?

Mr. McIntosh: Well, of course, the definition of prurient is: disposed to lewdness.

The Court:. Or exciting impure sexual thoughts.

Mr. McIntosh: Lascivious thoughts.

The Court: That would excite a person to lewd or lascivious thoughts, impure sexual thoughts.

Mr. McIntosh: Of course, the people's contention, your Honor, is that the obscenity goes further than that. Otherwise, it would not be against the law to write these words anywhere you felt like it.

The Court: Well, can you comply with my request?

Mr. McIntosh: How about page 136?

The Court: All right. If you'll read the passage that you are referring to.

Mr. McIntosh: All right. Down at the bottom: "Who sweetened the snatches of a million girls trembling in the sunset," and the next one, a little further, after "Adonis of Denver"—"Joy to the memory of his innumerable lays of girls in empty lots." Two at the moment, your Honor.

Page 26: "I remember when I first got laid, H.P.—" whoever that is—"graciously took my cherry, I sat on the docks of Provincetown, age 23, joyful, elevated in hope with the father, the door to the womb was open to admit me if I wished to enter."

That's three at the moment, your Honor.

The Court: All right. Now, let me ask you this question: Have you read Ulysses?

Mr. McIntosh: I have not, your Honor. I might make this other observation, your Honor. If this were a jury trial, certainly the jury would not be able to compare books and I don't think we have any right to compare any of these books here to the one in issue.

The Court: I am afraid you are wrong, Mr. McIntosh. In the trial of "Hecate County" here in San Francisco, it's my recollection that there were other books submitted to the jury for comparison.

Mr. McIntosh: Never went up on appeal, your Honor.

The Court: I know it didn't go up on appeal. That's not the only trial. I can't put my finger on a citation now, but you'll find there are other cases where books were submitted to juries for comparison purposes.

Mr. McIntosh: Oh, I had a whole load of them in the last case I tried, your Honor. That was the case with the nudist books. They had everything but the bible in there.

The Court: Well, there are a number of cases that hold that books may be submitted to the jury for comparison purposes. All right, I will hear from the defense.

Mr. Ehrlich: Your Honor, if it please you, on page 79 of the record, you said:

"We have to go back to the basis that the book and its contents are to be construed as a whole. In addition to that, the sentence you just read, as you read it, has nothing in it that smacks or savors of eroticism or vulgar language. Now, it may be unusual language but there's nothing in there that contains either of those elements and certainly I can hold that as a matter of law. Now, if you have any particular words that you think are capable of inducing lustful thoughts or depraving anyone or inciting them to commit depraved acts as the result of reading these particular passages or words, or if you think there are some in there that are vulgar to the point of being pornographic, you may direct the witness to them along the lines that we have previously discussed as to whether or not they are relative to the theme and to the vehicle itself. But the question that you have just put will not be allowed because you could go through this book line by line and it would be a waste of time and not relevant to the question that's before the court, to wit: Is the vehicle or book as a whole obscene?"

That is a correct, and clear statement of the law. The United States Supreme Court has said that obscenity is construed to mean having a substantial tendency to corrupt by arousing lustful desires. I read from the Pennsylvania case of Gordon versus Commonwealth:

"It is because Joyce has been loyal to his technique and has not funked its necessary implications, but has honestly attempted to tell fully what his characters think about, that he has been the subject of so many attacks and that his purpose has been so often misunderstood and misrepresented. For his attempt sincerely and honestly to realize his objective has required him incidentally to use certain words which are generally considered dirty words and has led at times to what many think is a too poignant preoccupation with sex in the thoughts of his character.

"The words which are criticized as dirty are old, Saxon words known to almost all men and, I venture, to many women, and are such words as would be naturally and habitually used, I believe, by the types of folk whose life, physical and mental, Joyce is seeking to describe. As I have stated, 'Ulysses' is not an easy book to read. It is brilliant and dull, intelligible and obscure, by turns. In many places it seems to me to be disgusting, but although it contains, as I have mentioned above, many words, usually considered dirty, I have not found anything that I considered to be dirt for dirt's sake. Each word of the book contributes like a bit of Mosaic to the detail of the picture which Joyce is seeking to construct for his readers.

"If one does not wish to associate with such folk as Joyce describes, that is one's own choice. In order to avoid indirect contact with them, one may not wish to read 'Ulysses'; that is quite understandable. But when such a great artist in words, as Joyce undoubtedly is, seeks to draw a true picture of the lower middle-class in a European City, ought it to be impossible for the American public legally to see that picture?"

And in affirming Judge Woolsey, Judge Hand said:

"That numerous long passages in Ulysses contain matter that is obscene under any fair definition of the word cannot be gainsaid; yet they are relevant to the purpose of depicting the thoughts of the characters and are introduced to give meaning to the whole, rather than to promote lust or portray filth for its own sake. The net effect even of portions most open to attack, such as the closing monologue of the wife of Leopold Bloom, is pitiful and tragic, rather than lustful. The book depicts the souls of men and women that are by turns bewildered and keenly apprehensive, sordid and aspiring, ugly and beautiful, hateful and loving. In the end one feels, more than anything else, pity and sorrow for the confusion, misery, and degradation of humanity. The book as a whole is not pornographic, and, while in not a few spots it is coarse, blasphemous, and obscene, it does not, in our opinion, tend to promote lust. The erotic passages are submerged in the books as a whole and have little resultant effect."

In our case much has been made by the prosecution concerning the four-letter word, and there's been hesitance on the part of the District Attorney to use the word. I, for one, see nothing wrong with the word since it is a word commonly used in the English language, and was used up to and past the time of Queen Elizabeth. It is a plain, common Anglo-Saxon word meaning "to plant." This word is known to all and it has been used in some beautiful poetry. I will read to Your Honor by way of illustration three stanzas from a poem by Christopher Marlowe, who lived between 1564 and 1593. If we believe what some have written, Shakespeare copied several of Christopher Marlowe's great dramas. Marlowe wrote:

"I love thee not for Sacred Chastity.
Who loves for that? Nor for thy sprightly wit:
I love thee not for thy sweet modesty,
Which makes thee in perfection's throne to sit.
I love thee not for thy enchanting eye,
Thy beauty, ravishing perfection:
I love thee not for that my soul doth dance,
And leap with pleasure when those lips of thine,
Give musical and graceful utterance,
To some (by thee made happy) Poet's line
I love thee not for voice or slender small,
But wilt thee know wherefore? Fair sweet, for all.
'Faith Wench! I cannot court thy sprightly eyes
With the base viol placed between my thighs;
I cannot lisp, nor to some fiddle sing,
Nor run upon a high minikin.
I cannot whine in puling elegies.
Entombing cupid with sad obsequies:
I am not fashioned for these amorous times,
To court thy beauty with lascivious rhymes:

I cannot dally, caper, dance and sing,
Oiling my saint with supple sonneting:
I cannot cross my arms, or sigh, "Ah me,"
"Ah me forlorn!" Egregious foppery!
I cannot buss thy fill, play with thy hair,
Swearing by Jove, "Thou art most debonnaire!"
Not I, by cock! But I shall tell thee roundly,
Hark in thine ear, zounds I can fuck thee soundly."

That was written by one of England's greatest poets. There are those who, when they read, attribute everything wrong and improper to what they read because mentally they want it to be that way. You do not think common, lewd or lascivious thoughts just because you have read something in a book, unless it is your mental purpose to do so. Impure sexual thoughts or prurient interest is self-generated by a desiring mind which is disposed to lewdness and impure sexual thoughts.

The prosecution confuses this work with the question raised in Roth versus United States. In the Roth case there was a pornographic work advertised, sent through the mails, sold with advertising suggesting lewd sexual relationships. We do not have any such thing here. Would we, if he were alive today, arrest Christopher Marlowe for writing his poem because Mr. Kirk suggests it? The four letter word "fuck" is not used in our work to cater to prurient interest.

The Court: May I interrupt you there for a minute? I don't think you contend that that word is used in so-called polite society, do you?

Mr. Ehrlich: Well, I don't know what your Honor means by "polite society." Polite society? Are there degrees?

The Court: In other words, if you were invited to a party, would you use that word while discussing something with someone there, some ladies, for example?

Mr. Ehrlich: I do not think that the mere use of one word

is going to destroy anyone's morals or cause them to embrace that which is base and unworthy of an intellect of decency.

The Court: No, I am not approaching it from that standpoint. I am approaching it from the standpoint that—let me ask you this question: Are you willing to concede that there are certain words in "Howl" that generally at this time, in this place—I don't mean this courtroom; I mean in the community—may be considered coarse and vulgar?

Mr. Ehrlich: Yes, I will concede that they may be so considered. I can't visualize the use of so-called discolored words, whether acceptable or unacceptable unless they are relevant to the theme. Our problem is whether these words are relevant to the theme of the book and not where and when we should use these words. As has been aptly said, a word is not a crystal, transparent and unchanged. It is the skin of a living thought and may vary greatly in color and content according to the circumstances and the time in which it is used. Is the word relevant to what the author is saying, or did he use it just to be dirty and filthy? In Howl, is it relevant to what he is saying when Ginsberg cries out:

"America I've given you all and now I'm nothing.
America two dollars and twenty seven cents January 17, 1956
I can't stand on my own mind.
America when will we end the human war?

He then answers the threat, he says:

"Go fuck yourself with your atom bomb.
I don't feel good don't bother me."

What prurient interest is Ginsberg generating with that cry of pain? This man is at the end of the road. He is crying out in the wilderness. Nobody is listening. Your Honor can't feel that anguished cry nor can I. We cannot understand it. We have never lived his life. A man doesn't know the pain of a toothache unless he has a toothache. In love with your wife and devoted to her, you still cannot share or feel her toothache.

We do not know what Ginsberg's mind was saying at the moment he wrote these lines because we haven't experienced hunger; we haven't reached the bottom of the pit. And who can say what a man would say or do in any given set of circumstances.

Mr. McIntosh referred to the top of page 133 where Ginsberg is telling us in his howl for Carl Solomon that:

"I saw the best minds of my generation destroyed
    by madness, starving hysterical naked,
Dragging themselves through the negro streets at
    dawn looking for an angry fix."

And he continues describing what is going on. He keeps talking about what he sees. He sees endless subways from the Battery to the Bronx, benzedrine, noise of wheels, "Battered bleak of brain all drained of brilliance," "a lost battalion," "screaming vomiting whispering facts and memories and anecdotes" "whole intellects disgorged in total recall," "meet for the Synagogue cast on the pavement," he continues describing the man who studied philosophy, "studied St. John of the Cross," the Kaballa "who jumped in limousines with the Chinaman of Oklahoma," "who lounged hungry and lonesome through Houston seeking jazz or sex or soup," seeking, seeking, seeking, always, broken down, crying, everything is wrong with him, they do everything Solomon is doing, everything he ought not to do, he associates with millions of girls, "red-eyed in the morning but prepared to sweeten the snatch of the sunrise, flashing buttocks under barns and naked in the lake," he goes on through Colorado, sees what he terms as the "Adonis of Denver," joy to the memory of his innumerable conquests. Instead of saying "innumerable conquests," he says "Lays of girls in empty lots and diner back-yards, moviehouses, rickety rows on mountaintops."

After reciting all this turmoil and all he had seen, he could have said that the secret hero of these poems, this cocksman, an Adonis of Denver, joy to memory of his innumerable conquests in the Waldorf Astoria, in dinner at Chasen's, and a drink or two before going to bed in the Stork Club. I presume he could have said that, but that isn't the type of people he was talking about; he was talking here about Solomon, this figurative man who marches through all this turmoil and degradation.

If the prosecution can say, that because Adonis laid girls in empty lots and movie houses and on mountaintops and in caves, makes this book an obscene book, then the law and the decisions are valueless. It isn't for us to choose the words. When Ginsberg tells his story, he tells it as he sees it, uses the words as he knows them, and portrays in his language that which he sees.

And another place referred to by Mr. McIntosh: "The kichen has no door, the hole there will admit me should I wish to enter the kitchen.

> "I remember when I first got laid, H. P. graciously took my cherry, I sat on the docks of Provincetown, age 23, joyful, elevated in the hope with the Father,—" capitalized—"The door to the womb was open to admit me if I wished to enter."

I can show your Honor passages in the Bible that describe what this man is thinking and much clearer than he has said it. What is wrong? What creates lewd and lascivious thoughts in the fact that the man has come to a realization of one of the natural urges of life, which is the opening of an entire new world to him, and he says it and says it reverently, "elevated in hope with the Father." What in that, may I ask the prosecution, will destroy mankind? I find nothing that is salacious, filthy, dirty, lewd, lascivious or licentious.

There is no evidence of any obscenity. I can find no evidence here of any salacious appeal nor is there any evidence of anything which urges that the book be bought and read on account of it.

There is no evidence of the lewd intent required by the law. There is no evidence that defendant sold this book lewdly. The prosecution sought to make the point that the book was published by the City Lights Pocket Bookshop. That's what it says, but that isn't enough, your Honor. There must be something else. The mere fact that the man published it, the mere fact that he sold it is not enough. There must be something else. There must be some act on his part. Mr. Chief Justice Warren says that first a man is on trial. What was his conduct in relation to the book? Did he sell it for the purpose of creating lewd interests? Did he sell it in order to urge and awaken the prurient desires and purpose and interests of others? The only evidence before this Court is that a police officer bought this book.

The Court: Stopping you there for a moment, it has been proved that the book was published by the City Lights Bookshop, and the testimony is also in the record that the defendant Ferlinghetti is the owner of the City Lights Bookshop. So, therefore, he published it. And that there was no one else on the premises at the time he sold it, so the only charge against the defendant Ferlinghetti would be confined to publishing and keeping for sale.

Mr. Ehrlich: The law is that the mere sale or the keeping of a prohibited book will support an inference that the defendant acted lewdly only if there is some evidence that he knew the book to be obscene in character. That is the only time that this inference can be drawn. Your Honor will recall that we introduced reviews from magazines and newspapers, each of which praised "Howl" and not one called it obscene.

The defendant could and did rely on the opinion of those who are qualified to weigh the literary merit of a writing or book.

Mr. McIntosh inquired whether the Court would like to have "Howl" read over the radio or on television. While it is not in the record, I inform the Court that it has been televised and broadcast on Station KPFA. It is a book that has been highly publicized as the result of this trial, and has been discussed in literary groups who were not interested in this new Howl of human pain.

Your Honor, what shall I quote to convey the thought that great works and classics of literature are at first condemned by those who see destruction in everything they cannot understand and find pornographic skeletons in every closet?

I point out that Voltaire's Candide was originally condemned as obscene because it dealt with sex. But even the prosecution's star witness says that this work is a classic. Words dealing with and describing sex do not destroy literary merit.

Shall we cull the lines from Balzac's stories? Shall we forthwith ban his works, take the volumes from the library shelves and hide behind the barn to read? Seek filth and you will find it. Seek beauty of narration and you will find that too. But to find filth you must search for it with a wanton mind and a willing application.

Any book can be declared unsafe since a moron could pervert to some sexual fantasy to which his mind is open the listings in a seed catalogue. Not even the Bible would be exempt; Annie Besant once compiled a list of 150 passages in Scripture that might fairly be considered obscene—it is enough to cite the story of Lot and his daughters, Genesis 19, 30–38. Portions of Shakespeare would also be offensive and of Chaucer, to say nothing of Aristophanes, Juvenal, Ovid, Swift, Defoe, Fielding, Smollett, Rousseau, Maupassant, Voltaire, Balzac, Baudelaire, Rabelais, Swinburne, Shelley,

Byron, Boccaccio, Marguerite de Naverre, Hardy, Shaw, Whitman, and a host more.

Mr. Kirk testified that copying does not produce literature. He must have overlooked the Jew of Malta, a tragic drama by Christopher Marlowe written about 1590 and anticipating Shakespeare's The Merchant of Venice in plot. Much of the plot of the Merchant of Venice first appeared in the Gesta Romanorum in the 14th Century.

Now, your Honor, who copied whom, and who created literature? Perhaps our Mr. Kirk should not have limited his field of education.

There are books that have the power to change men's minds, and call attention to situations which are visible but unseen. Whether Howl is or is not "obscene" is of small importance in our world faced as it is with the problem of physical survival, but the problem of what is legally permissible in the description of sexual acts and feelings in art and literature is of the greatest importance in a free society.

It is generally established that the intention of a book as a whole, rather than the language of any particular passage, is the criterion of judging obscenity. There is not now, nor has there ever been a workable definition of obscenity. Every person will react to sex writings according to their own sexual tastes.

The so-called legal yardstick of "prurient" or "obscene" when applied to books is much like judging the color of a horse by how fast he can run. What is "prurient"? And to whom? "Prurient" it is said means "lewd," "lascivious" or some other synonym that defies precise definition. And the material so described is dangerous to some unspecified susceptible reader. It is interesting that the person applying such standards in censorship never feels that his own physical or moral health is in jeopardy. The desire to censor, however, is not limited to crackpots and bigots. There is in most of us a strong desire to make the world conform to our own ideas, and it takes all the force of our reason and our legal institutions to defy so human an urge. The courts have long wandered in a maze, and in their efforts to apply the concept of "contemporary community standards" have often appeared to be deciding matters of law by the watery drippings of public opinion.

No one wishes to give free license for the publication of obscene works. Yet the difficulties in deciding what is or is not obscene have forced many of us into extreme positions. The liberal sees the threat of censorship and would let everything pass to give freedom to what is good. Another man would risk the suppression of an occasional book to guard the community from what he considers the danger of obscene literature.

The battle of censorship will not be finally settled by your Honor's decision, but you will either add to liberal educated thinking or by your decision add fuel to the fire of ignorance.

I have seen the efforts of the prosecution to build up a case by counting four-letter words. I have seen the honest confusion of honest men trying to determine what is obscene with no real background of information to help them. I have seen the struggle with the semantic nonsense that is written into the law books as definitions of obscenity.

Let there be light. Let there be honesty. Let there be no running from non-existent destroyers of morals. Let there be honest understanding. In the end the four-letter words will not appear draped in glaring headlights, but will be submerged in the decentralization of small thinking in small minds.

Your Honor, Dr. Samuel Johnson could have been speaking of our self-appointed censor, when he describes Iago, the villain of Shakespeare's tragedy Othello, who deliberately strings together such a mass of circumstantial evidence in proof of Desdemona's love for Cassio, that the Moor kills her out of jealousy.

> "The cool malignity of Iago, silent in his
> resentment, subtle in his designs, and studious
> at once of his interest and his vengeance,"

to which I add, his ignorance.

The Court: Gentlemen, is the matter submitted?

Mr. McIntosh: Yes, your Honor.

Mr. Ehrlich: It may stand submitted.

The Court: October 3rd, at 2 P.M. for decision.

T H E
D E C I S I O N

HORN, CLAYTON W., J. The defendant is charged with a violation of Section 311.3 of the Penal Code of the State of California. Defendant pleads Not Guilty. The complaint alleged that the defendant did wilfully and lewdly print, publish and sell obscene and indecent writings, papers and books, to wit: "Howl and Other Poems."

It is to be noted that the statute requires proof of criminal intent, namely, that the defendants did wilfully and lewdly commit the acts specified. It should also be noted that no reference to minors is made in the statute.

It must be borne in mind that the prosecution has the burden of proving beyond a reasonable doubt and to a moral certainty two things: first, that the book is obscene and, second, that the defendants wilfully and lewdly committed the crime alleged. It is elementary that where a statute makes a specific intent an element of an offense, such intent must be proved. The proof may be circumstantial; but if so, the circumstances must be such as reasonably to justify an inference of the intent.

The prosecution has advanced the theory that the word "indecent" means something less than obscene.

In their broadest meaning the words indecent and obscene might signify offensive to refinement, propriety and good taste. A penal statute requiring conformity to some current standard of propriety defined only by statutory words would make the standard in each case, ex post facto.

Unless the words used take the form of dirt for dirt's sake and can be traced to criminal behavior, either actual or demonstrably imminent, they are not in violation of the statute. Indecent as used in the Penal Code is synonymous with obscene, and there is no merit in the contention of the prosecution that the word indecent means something less than obscene.

The evidence shows that "Howl" was published by the defendant and therefore it remains to be seen whether said book is obscene and if so, whether this defendant wilfully and lewdly published it. The prosecution contends that having published the book defendant had knowledge of the character of its contents and that from such knowledge a lewd intent might be inferred.

The mere fact of knowledge alone would not be sufficient. The surrounding circumstances would be important and must be such as reasonably to justify an inference of the intent. To illustrate, some might think a book obscene, others a work of art; with sincere difference of opinion. The bookseller would not be required to elect at his peril. Unless the prosecution proved that he acted lewdly in selling it, the burden would not be met.

Written reviews of "Howl" were admitted in evidence on behalf of the defendants, over the objection of the District Attorney. One was from The New York Times Book Review, dated September 2, 1956; one from the San Francisco Chronicle, dated May 19, 1957, which included a statement by Ferlinghetti; one from the Nation dated February 23, 1957. All of the reviews praised "Howl."

The practice of referring to reviews in cases of this nature has become well established. Opinions of professional critics publicly disseminated in the ordinary course of their employment are proper aids to the court in weighing the author's sincerity of purpose and the literary worth of his effort. These are factors which, while not determining whether a book is obscene, are to be considered in deciding that question.

Over the objection of the prosecution the defense produced nine expert witnesses, some of them with outstanding qualifications in the literary field. All of the defense experts agreed that "Howl" had literary merit, that it represented a sincere effort by the author to present a social picture, and that the language used was relevant to the theme. As Professor Mark Schorer put it: "Howl," like any work of literature, attempts and intends to make a significant comment on, or interpretation of, human experience as the author knows it.

The prosecution produced two experts in rebuttal, whose qualifications were slightly less than those of the defense. One testified that "Howl" had some clarity of thought but was an imitation of Walt Whitman, and had no literary merit; the other and by far the most voluble, that it had no value at all. The court did not allow any of the experts to express an opinion on the question of obscenity because this was the very issue to be decided by the court.

Experts are used every day in court on other subjects and no reason presents itself justifying their exclusion from this type of case when their experience and knowledge can be of assistance. The court also read many of the books previously held obscene or not for the purpose of comparison.

In determining whether a book is obscene it must be construed as a whole. The courts are agreed that in making this determination, the book must be construed as a whole and that regard shall be had for its place in the arts.

The freedoms of speech and press are inherent in a nation of free people. These freedoms must be protected if we are to remain free, both individually and as a nation. The protection for this freedom is found in the First and Fourteenth Amendments to the United States Constitution, and in the Constitution of California, Art. I, sec. 9 which provides in part:

"Every citizen may freely speak, write, and publish his sentiments on all subjects, being responsible for the abuse of that right; and no law shall be passed to restrain or abridge the liberty of speech or of the press . . ."

The Fourteenth Amendment to the Federal Constitution prohibts any State from encroaching upon freedom of speech and freedom of the press to the same extent that the First Amendment prevents the Federal Congress from doing so.

These guarantees occupy a preferred position under our law to such an extent that the courts, when considering whether legislation infringes upon them, neutralize the presumption usually indulged in favor of constitutionality.

Thomas Jefferson in his bill for establishing religious freedom wrote that "to suffer the Civil Magistrate to intrude his powers into the field of opinion, and to restrain the profession or propagation of principles on supposition of their ill tendency, is a dangerous fallacy which at once destroys all religious liberty . . . it is time enough for the rightful purposes of civil government for its officers to interfere when principles break out into overt acts against peace and good order."

The now familiar "clear and present danger" rule represents a compromise between the ideas of Jefferson and those of the judges, who had in the meantime departed from the forthright views of the great statesman. Under the rule the publisher of a writing may be punished if the publication in question creates a clear and present danger that there will result from it some substantive evil which the legislature has a right to proscribe and punish.

Mr. Justice Brandeis maintained that free speech may not be curbed where the community has the chance to answer back. He said: "those who won our independence by revolution were not cowards. They did not fear political change. They did not exalt order at the cost of liberty. To courageous, self-reliant men, with confidence in the power of free and fearless reasoning applied through the processes of popular government, no danger flowing from speech can be deemed clear and present, unless the incidence of the evil apprehended is so imminent that it may befall before there is opportunity for full discussion. If there be time to expose through discussion the falsehood and fallacies, to avert the evil by the processes of education, the remedy to be applied is more speech, not enforced silence. Only an emergency can justify repression. Such must be the rule if authority is to be reconciled with freedom. Such, in my opinion, is the command of the Constitution. It is therefore always open to Americans to challenge a law abridging free speech and assembly by showing that there was no emergency justifying it.

"Moreover, even imminent danger cannot justify resort to prohibition of these functions essential to effective democracy, unless the evil apprehended is relatively serious. Prohibition of free speech and assembly is a measure so stringent that it would be inappropriate as the means for averting a relatively trivial harm to society—the fact that speech is likely to result in some violence or in destruction of property is not enough to justify its suppression. There must be the probability of serious injury to the State. Among free men, the deterrents ordinarily to be applied to prevent crime are education and punishment for violations of the law, not abridgment of the rights of free speech and assembly."

The authors of the First Amendment knew that novel and unconventional ideas might disturb the complacent, but they chose to encourage a freedom which they believed essential if vigorous enlightenment was ever to triumph over slothful ignorance.

I agree with the words of Macaulay who finds it difficult to believe that in a world so full of temptations as this, any gentleman, whose life would have been virtuous if he had not read Aristophanes and Juvenal, will be made vicious by reading them.

I do not believe that "Howl" is without redeeming social importance. The first part of "Howl" presents a picture of a nightmare world; the second part is an indictment of those elements in modern society destructive of the best qualities of human nature; such elements are predominantly identified as materialism, conformity, and mechanization leading toward war. The third part presents a picture of an individual who is a specific representation of what the author conceives as a general condition.

"Footnote to Howl" seems to be a declamation that everything in the world is holy, including parts of the body by name. It ends in a plea for holy living.

The poems, "Supermarket," "Sunflower Sutra," "In the Baggage Room at Greyhound," "An Asphodel," "Song" and "Wild Orphan" require no discussion relative to obscenity. In "Transcription of Organ Music" the "I" in four lines remembers his first sex relation at age 23 but only the bare ultimate fact and that he enjoyed it. Even out of context it is written in language that is not obscene, and included in the whole it becomes a part of the individual's experience "real or imagined," but lyric rather than hortatory and violent, like "Howl."

The theme of "Howl" presents "unorthodox and controversial ideas." Coarse and vulgar language is used in treatment and sex acts are mentioned, but unless the book is entirely lacking in "social importance" it cannot be held obscene. This point does not seem to have been specifically presented or decided in any of the cases leading up to Roth v. United States.

No hard and fast rule can be fixed for the determination of what is obscene, because such determination depends on the locale, the time, the mind of the community and the prevailing mores. Even the word itself has had a chameleon-like history through the past, and as Mr. Justice Cardozo said: "A word is not a crystal, transparent and unchanged. It is the skin of living thought and may vary greatly in color and content according to the circumstances and the time in which it is used." The writing, however, must have a substantial tendency to deprave or corrupt its readers by inciting lascivious thoughts or arousing lustful desires.

The effect of the publication on the ordinary reader is what counts. The Statute does not intend that we shall "reduce our treatment of sex to the standard of a child's library in the supposed interest of a salacious few. This test, however, should not be left to stand alone, for there is another element of equal importance—the tenor of the times and the change in social acceptance of what is inherently decent.

The modern rule is that obscenity is measured by the erotic allurement upon the average modern reader; that the erotic allurement of a book is measured by whether it is sexually impure—i.e., pornographic, "dirt for dirt's sake," a calculated incitement to sexual desire—or whether it reveals an effort to reflect life, including its dirt, with reasonable accuracy and balance; and that mere coarseness or vulgarity is not obscenity.

Sexual impurity in literature (pornography, as some of the cases call it) is any writing whose dominant purpose and effect is erotic allurement; a calculated and effective incitement to sexual desire. It is the effect that counts, more than the purpose, and no indictment can stand unless it can be shown.

In the Roth case no question of obscenity was involved or considered by the court. The sole question was whether obscenity as such was protected by the constitution and the court held it was not. In the appeals involved the material was obviously pornographic, it was advertised and sold as such. The United States Supreme Court refers to the various rules on obscenity by stating that: "sex and obscenity are not synonymous. Obscene material is material which deals with sex in a manner appealing to prurient interest. The portrayal of sex, e.g., in art, literature and scientific works is not itself sufficient reason to deny material the constitutional protection of freedom of speech and press."

The following instruction, given in the Alberts case, is approved in Roth: "The test is not whether it would arouse sexual desires or sexual impure thoughts in those comprising a particular segment of the community, the young, the immature or the highly prudish, or would leave another segment, the scientific or highly educated or the so-called worldly-wise and sophisticated indifferent and unmoved. The test in each case is the effect of the book, picture or publication considered as a whole, not upon any particular class, but upon all those whom it is likely to reach. In other words, you determine its impact upon the average person in the community. The books, pictures and circulars must be judged, as a whole, in their entire context, and you are not to consider detached or separate portions in reaching a conclusion. You judge the circulars, pictures and publications which have been put in evidence by present-day standards of the community. You may ask yourself does it offend the common conscience of the community by present-day standards. In this case, ladies and gentlemen of the jury, you and you alone are the exclusive judges of what the common conscience of the community is, and in determining that conscience you are to consider the community as a whole, young and old,

educated and uneducated, the religous and the irreligious—
men, women and children."

Mr. Chief Justice Warren, concurring in the result in the
Roth case, stated: "I agree with the result reached by the
court in these cases, but the line dividing the salacious or
pornographic from literature or science is not straight and
unwavering, the personal element in these cases is seen most
strongly in the requirement of scienter. Under the California
law, the prohibited activity must be done 'wilfully and
lewdly.' "

There are a number of words used in "Howl" that are
presently considered coarse and vulgar in some circles of the
community; in other circles such words are in everyday use.
It would be unrealistic to deny these facts. The author of
"Howl" has used those words because he believed that his
portrayal required them as being in character. The People
state that it is not necessary to use such words and that others
would be more palatable to good taste. The answer is that
life is not encased in one formula whereby everyone acts the
same or conforms to a particular pattern. No two persons
think alike; we were all made from the same mold but in
different patterns. Would there be any freedom of press or
speech if one must reduce his vocabulary to vapid innocuous
euphemism? An author should be real in treating his subject
and be allowed to express his thoughts and ideas in his own
words.

In People v. Viking Press, the court said: "The Courts have
strictly limited the applicability of the statute to works of
pornography and they have consistently declined to apply it
to books of genuine literary value. If the statute were construed more broadly than in the manner just indicated, its
effect would be to prevent altogether the realistic portrayal
in literature of a large and important field of life. . . . The
Court may not require the author to put refined language
into the mouths of primitive people," and in People v. Van-

guard Press, the court observed: "The speech of the characters must be considered in relation to its setting and the theme of the story. It seems clear that use of foul language will not of itself bring a novel or play within the condemnation of the statute. As I have indicated above, all but one of these books are profoundly tragic, and that one has its normal quota of frustration and despair. No one could envy or wish to emulate the characters that move so desolately through these pages. Far from inciting to lewd or lecherous desires, which are sensorially pleasurable, these books leave one either with a sense of horror or of pity for the degradation of mankind. The effect upon the normal reader, *l'homme moyen sensuel* (there is no such deft precision in English), would be anything but what the vice hunters fear it might be. We are so fearful for other people's morals; they so seldom have the courage of our own convictions."

In Commonwealth v. Gordon: the test for obscenity most frequently laid down seems to be whether the writing would tend to deprave the morals of those into whose hands the publication might fall by suggesting lewd thoughts and exciting sensual desires. The statute is therefore directed only at sexual impurity and not at blasphemy or coarse and vulgar behavior of any other kind. The word in common use for the purpose of such statute is "obscenity." The familiar four-letter words that are so often associated with sexual impurity are, almost without exception, of honest Anglo-Saxon ancestry, and were not invented for purely scatological effect. The one, for example, that is used to denote the sexual act is an old agricultural word meaning "to plant" and was at one time a wholly respectable member of the English vocabulary. The distinction between a word of decent etymological history and one of smut alone is important; it shows that fashions in language change as expectably as do the concepts of what language connotes. It is the old business of semantics again, the difference between word and concept. But there is another distinction. The decisions that I cite have sliced off vulgarity from obscenity. This has had the effect of making a clear division between the words of the bathroom and those of the bedroom; the former can no longer be regarded as obscene, since they have no erotic allurement, and the latter may be so regarded, depending on the circumstances of their use. This reduces the number of potentially offensive words sharply.

"The law does not undertake to punish bad English, vulgarity, or bad taste, and no matter how objectionable one may consider the book on those grounds, there is no right to convict on account of them. The dramatization of the song 'Frankie and Johnnie' caused much furor, but the court there held that 'the language of the play is coarse, vulgar and profane; the plot cheap and tawdry. As a dramatic composition it serves to degrade the stage where vice is thought by some to lose "half its evil by losing all its grossness." That it is indecent from every consideration of propriety is entirely clear' but the court is not a censor of plays and does not attempt to regulate manners. One may call a spade a spade without offending decency, although modesty may be shocked thereby. The question is not whether the scene is laid in a low dive where refined people are not found or whether the language is that of the bar room rather than the parlor. The question is whether the tendency of the play is to excite lustful and lecherous desire."

To determine whether a book falls within the condemnation of the statute, an evaluation must be made of the extent to which the book as a whole would have a demoralizing effect on its readers, specifically respecting sexual behavior. Various factors must be borne in mind when applying the judicially accepted standards used in measuring that effect. Among others, these factors include the theme of the book, the degree of sincerity of purpose evidenced in it, its literary worth, the channels used in its distribution, contemporary attitudes toward the literary treatment of sexual behavior and the types of readers reasonably to be expected to secure it for perusal.

Material is not obscene unless it arouses lustful thoughts of sex and tends to corrupt and deprave *l'homme moyen sensuel* by inciting him to anti-social activity or tending to create a clear and present danger that he will be so incited as the result of exposure thereto.

If the material is disgusting, revolting or filthy, to use just a few adjectives, the antithesis of pleasurable sexual desires is born, and it cannot be obscene.

In United States v. Roth, a footnote to the concurring opinion of Judge Frank is of interest: "The very argument advanced to sustain the statute's validity, so far as it condemns the obscene, goes to show the invalidity of the statute so far as it condemns 'filth,' if 'filth' means that which renders sexual desires 'disgusting.' For if the argument be sound that the legislature may constitutionally provide punishment for the obscene because, anti-socially, it arouses sexual desires by making sex attractive, then it follows that whatever makes sex disgusting is socially beneficial.

"To date there exist, I think, no thoroughgoing studies by competent persons which justify the conclusion that normal adults reading or seeing of the 'obscene' probably induces anti-social conduct. Such competent studies as have been made do conclude that so complex and numerous are the causes of sexual vice that it is impossible to assert with any assurance that 'obscenity' represents a ponderable causal factor in sexually deviant behavior. Although the whole subject of obscenity censorship hinges upon the unproved assumption that 'obscene' literature is a significant factor in causing sexual deviation from the community standard, no report can be found of a single effort at genuine research to test this assumption by singling out as a factor for study the effect of sex literature upon sexual behavior. What little competent research has been done, points definitely in a direction precisely opposite to that assumption."

While the publishing of "smut" or "hard core pornography" is without any social importance and obscene by present-day standards, and should be punished for the good of the community, since there is no straight and unwavering line to act as a guide, censorship by Government should be held in tight reign. To act otherwise would destroy our freedoms of free speech and press. Even religion can be censored by the medium of taxation. The best method of censorship is by the people as self-guardians of public opinion and not by government. So we come back, once more, to Jefferson's advice that the only completely democratic way to control publications which arouse mere thoughts or feelings is through non-governmental censorship by public opinion.

From the foregoing certain rules can be set up, but as has been noted, they are not inflexible and are subject to changing conditions, and above all each case must be judged individually.

1. If the material has the slightest redeeming social importance it is not obscene because it is protected by the First and Fourteenth Amendments of the United States Constitution, and the California Constitution.

2. If it does not have the slightest redeeming social importance it may be obscene.

3. The test of obscenity in California is that the material must have a tendency to deprave or corrupt readers by exciting lascivious thoughts or arousing lustful desire to the point that it presents a clear and present danger of inciting to anti-social or immoral action.

4. The book or material must be judged as a whole by its effect on the *average adult* in the community.

5. If the material is objectionable only because of coarse and vulgar language which is not erotic or aphrodisiac in character it is not obscene.

6. Scienter must be proved.

7. Book reviews may be received in evidence if properly authenticated.

8. Evidence of expert witnesses in the literary field is proper.

9. Comparison of the material with other similar material previously adjudicated is proper.

10. The people owe a duty to themselves and to each other to preserve and protect their constitutional freedoms from any encroachment by government unless it appears that the allowable limits of such protection have been breached, and then to take only such action as will heal the breach.

11. I agree with Mr. Justice Douglas: I have the same confidence in the ability of our people to reject noxious literature as I have in their capacity to sort out the true from the false in theology, economics, politics, or any other field.

12. In considering material claimed to be obscene it is well to remember the motto: *"Honi soit qui mal y pense."* (Evil to him who evil thinks.)

Therefore, I conclude the book "Howl and Other Poems" does have some redeeming social importance, and I find the book is not obscene.

The defendant is found not guilty.

BIBLIOGRAPHY OF THE ARGUMENT AND THE DECISION

California Constitution, Art. I, sec. 9.

45 Calif. L. Rev. 70.

California Penal Code, sec. 311.

Commonwealth v. Gordon, 66 Pa. D. & C. R. 101.

Commonwealth v. Isenstadt, 62 N. E. 2nd 840.

People v. Creative Age Press, 79 N.Y.S. 2d 198.

People v. Vanguard Press, 192 N.Y. misc. 127.

People v. Viking Press, 147 N.Y. misc. 813.

People v. Vogel, 46 Cal. App. 2d Supp. 959.
People v. Wepplo, 78 Cal. App. 2d Supp. 959; 178 P. 2d 853.
Roth v. United States, 354 U.S. 476.
Sweezy v. State of New Hampshire, 354 U.S. 234.
United States Constitution, First and Fourteenth Amendments.
United States v. Roth, 237 Fed. 2d 796 (C.C.A.).
Watkins v. United States, 354 U.S. 178.
Yates v. United States, 354 U.S. 298.

Extract from
HOWL AND OTHER POEMS
by Allen Ginsberg
Including the Introduction by
William Carlos Williams, HOWL
and FOOTNOTE TO HOWL

HOWL FOR CARL SOLOMON

When he was younger, and I was younger, I used to know Allen Ginsberg, a young poet living in Paterson, New Jersey, where he, son of a well-known poet, had been born and grew up. He was physically slight of build and mentally much disturbed by the life which he had encountered about him during those first years after the first world war as it was exhibited to him in and about New York City. He was always on the point of "going away," where it didn't seem to matter; he disturbed me, I never thought he'd live to grow up and write a book of poems. His ability to survive, travel, and go on writing astonishes me. That he has gone on developing and perfecting his art is no less amazing to me.

Now he turns up fifteen or twenty years later with an arresting poem. Literally he has, from all the evidence, been through hell. On the way he met a man named Carl Solomon with whom he shared among the teeth and excrement of this life something that cannot be described but in the words he has used to describe it. It is a howl of defeat. Not defeat at all for he has gone through defeat as if it were an ordinary experience, a trivial experience. Everyone in this life is defeated but a man, if he be a man, is not defeated.

It is the poet, Allen Ginsberg, who has gone, in his own body, through the horrifying experiences described from life in these pages. The wonder of the thing is not that he has survived but that he, from the very depths, has found a fellow whom he can love, a love he celebrates without looking aside in these poems. Say what you will, he proves to us, in spite of the most debasing experiences that life can offer a man, the spirit of love survives to ennoble our lives if we have the wit and the courage and the faith—and the art! to persist.

It is the belief in the art of poetry that has gone hand in hand with this man into his Golgotha, from that charnel house, similar in every way, to that of the Jews in the past war. But this is in our own country, our own fondest purlieus. We are blind and live our blind lives out in blindness. Poets are damned but they are not blind, they see with the eyes of the angels. This poet sees through and all around the horrors he partakes of in the very intimate details of his poem. He avoids nothing but experiences it to the hilt. He contains it. Claims it as his own—and, we believe, laughs at it and has the time and effrontery to love a fellow of his choice and record that love in a well-made poem.

Hold back the edges of your gowns, Ladies, we are going through hell.

WILLIAM CARLOS WILLIAMS

H O W L

for Carl Solomon

BY ALLEN GINSBERG

I

I saw the best minds of my generation destroyed by madness,
    starving hysterical naked,
dragging themselves through the negro streets at dawn looking
    for an angry fix,
angelheaded hipsters burning for the ancient heavenly connec-
    tion to the starry dynamo in the machinery of night,
who poverty and tatters and hollow-eyed and high sat up smok-
    ing in the supernatural darkness of cold-water flats float-
    ing across the tops of cities contemplating jazz,
who bared their brains to Heaven under the El and saw Moham-
    medan angels staggering on tenement roofs illuminated,
who passed through universities with radiant cool eyes halluci-
    nating Arkansas and Blake-light tragedy among the
    scholars of war,
who were expelled from the academies for crazy & publishing
    obscene odes on the windows of the skull,
who cowered in unshaven rooms in underwear, burning their
    money in wastebaskets and listening to the Terror
    through the wall,
who got busted in their public beards returning through Laredo
    with a belt of marijuana for New York,
who ate fire in paint hotels or drank turpentine in Paradise
    Alley, death, or purgatoried their torsos night after night
with dreams, with drugs, with waking nightmares, alcohol and
    cock and endless balls,

incomparable blind streets of shuddering cloud and lightning in
       the mind leaping toward poles of Canada & Paterson,
       illuminating all the motionless world of Time between,
Peyote solidities of halls, backyard green tree cemetery dawns,
       wine drunkenness over the rooftops, storefront boroughs
       of teahead joyride neon binking traffic light, sun and
       moon and tree vibrations in the roaring winter dusks of
       Brooklyn, ashcan rantings and kind king light of mind,
who chained themselves to subways for the endless ride from
       Battery to holy Bronx on benzedrine until the noise of
       wheels and children brought them down shuddering
       mouth-wracked and battered bleak of brain all drained
       of brilliance in the drear light of Zoo,
who sank all night in submarine light of Bickford's floated out
       and sat through the stale beer afternoon in desolate
       Fugazzi's, listening to the crack of doom on the hydrogen
       jukebox,
who talked continuously seventy hours from park to pad to bar
       to Bellevue to museum to the Brooklyn Bridge,
a lost battalion of platonic conversationalists jumping down the
       stoops off fire escapes off windowsills off Empire State
       out of the moon,
yacketayakking screaming vomiting whispering facts and mem-
       ories and anecdotes and eyeball kicks and shocks of
       hospitals and jails and wars,
whole intellects disgorged in total recall for seven days and
       nights with brilliant eyes, meat for the Synagogue cast
       on the pavement,
who vanished into nowhere Zen New Jersey leaving a trail of
       ambiguous picture postcards of Atlantic City Hall,
suffering Eastern sweats and Tangierian bone-grindings and
       migraines of China under junk-withdrawal in Newark's
       bleak furnished room,
who wandered around and around at midnight in the railroad
       yard wondering where to go, and went, leaving no
       broken hearts,
who lit cigarettes in boxcars boxcars boxcars racketing through
       snow toward lonesome farms in grandfather night,

who studied Plotinus Poe St. John of the Cross telepathy and
     bop kaballa because the cosmos instinctively vibrated
     at their feet in Kansas,

who loned it through the streets of Idaho seeking visionary
     indian angels who were visionary indian angels,

who thought they were only mad when Baltimore gleamed in
     supernatural ecstasy,

who jumped in limousines with the Chinaman of Oklahoma on
     the impulse of winter midnight streetlight smalltown
     rain,

who lounged hungry and lonesome through Houston seeking
     jazz or sex or soup, and followed the brilliant Spaniard
     to converse about America and Eternity, a hopeless task,
     and so took ship to Africa,

who disappeared into the volcanoes of Mexico leaving behind
     nothing but the shadow of dungarees and the lava and
     ash of poetry scattered in fireplace Chicago,

who reappeared on the West Coast investigating the F.B.I. in
     beards and shorts with big pacifist eyes sexy in their dark
     skin passing out incomprehensible leaflets,

who burned cigarette holes in their arms protesting the narcotic
     tobacco haze of Capitalism,

who distributed Supercommunist pamphlets in Union Square
     weeping and undressing while the sirens of Los Alamos
     wailed them down, and wailed down Wall, and the
     Staten Island ferry also wailed,

who broke down crying in white gymnasiums naked and trem-
     bling before the machinery of other skeletons,

who bit detectives in the neck and shrieked with delight in
     policecars for committing no crime but their own wild
     cooking pederasty and intoxication,

who howled on their knees in the subway and were dragged off
     the roof waving genitals and manuscripts,

who let themselves be . . . . . . in the . . . by saintly motor-
     cyclists, and screamed with joy,

who blew and were blown by those human seraphim, the sailors,
     caresses of Atlantic and Caribbean love,

who balled in the morning in the evenings in rosegardens and

the grass of public parks and cemeteries scattering their
semen freely to whomever come who may,

who hiccupped endlessly trying to giggle but wound up with a
sob behind a partition in a Turkish Bath when the blonde
& naked angel came to pierce them with a sword,

who lost their loveboys to the three old shrews of fate the one
eyed shrew of the heterosexual dollar the one eyed
shrew that winks out of the womb and the one eyed
shrew that does nothing but sit on her ass and snip the
intellectual golden threads of the craftsman's loom,

who copulated ecstatic and insatiate with a bottle of beer a
sweetheart a package of cigarettes a candle and fell off
the bed, and continued along the floor and down the
hall and ended fainting on the wall with a vision of ultimate c . . . and come eluding the last gyzym of consciousness,

who sweetened the snatches of a million girls trembling in the
sunset, and were red eyed in the morning but prepared
to sweeten the snatch of the sunrise, flashing buttocks
under barns and naked in the lake,

who went out whoring through Colorado in myriad stolen night-
cars, N.C., secret hero of these poems, cocksman and
Adonis of Denver—joy to the memory of his innumerable
lays of girls in empty lots & diner backyards, moviehouses, rickety rows on mountaintops in caves or with
gaunt waitresses in familiar roadside lonely petticoat
upliftings & especially secret gas-station solipsisms of
johns, & hometown alleys too,

who faded out in vast sordid movies, were shifted in dreams,
woke on a sudden Manhattan, and picked themselves up
out of basements hungover with heartless Tokay and
horrors of Third Avenue iron dreams & stumbled to un-
employment offices,

who walked all night with their shoes full of blood on the snow-
bank docks waiting for a door in the East River to open
to a room full of steamheat and opium,

who created great suicidal dramas on the apartment cliff-banks
of the Hudson under the wartime blue floodlight of the

moon & their heads shall be crowned with laurel in ob-
livion,

who ate the lamb stew of the imagination or digested the crab
at the muddy bottom of the rivers of Bowery,

who wept at the romance of the streets with their pushcarts full
of onions and bad music,

who sat in boxes breathing in the darkness under the bridge,
and rose up to build harpsichords in their lofts,

who coughed on the sixth floor of Harlem crowned with flame
under the tubercular sky surrounded by orange crates of
theology,

who scribbled all night rocking and rolling over lofty incanta-
tions which in the yellow morning were stanzas of
gibberish,

who cooked rotten animals lung heart feet tail borsht & tortillas
dreaming of the pure vegetable kingdom,

who plunged themselves under meat trucks looking for an egg,

who threw their watches off the roof to cast their ballot for
Eternity outside of Time, & alarm clocks fell on their
heads every day for the next decade,

who cut their wrists three times successively unsuccessfully, gave
up and were forced to open antique stores where they
thought they were growing old and cried,

who were burned alive in their innocent flannel suits on Madison
Avenue amid blasts of leaden verse & the tanked-up
clatter of the iron regiments of fashion & the nitroglycer-
ine shrieks of the fairies of advertising & the mustard gas
of sinister intelligent editors, or were run down by the
drunken taxicabs of Absolute Reality,

who jumped off the Brooklyn Bridge this actually happened and
walked away unknown and forgotten into the ghostly
daze of Chinatown soup alleyways & firetrucks, not even
one free beer,

who sang out of their windows in despair, fell out of the subway window, jumped in the filthy Passaic, leaped on
negroes, cried all over the street, danced on broken
wineglasses barefoot smashed phonograph records of
nostalgic European 1930's German jazz finished the

whiskey and threw up groaning into the bloody toilet, moans in their ears and the blast of colossal steam-whistles,

who barreled down the highways of the past journeying to each other's hotrod-Golgotha jail-solitude watch or Birmingham jazz incarnation,

who drove crosscountry seventytwo hours to find out if I had a vision or you had a vision or he had a vision to find out Eternity,

who journeyed to Denver, who died in Denver, who came back to Denver & waited in vain, who watched over Denver & brooded & loned in Denver and finally went away to find out the Time, & now Denver is lonesome for her heroes,

who fell on their knees in hopeless cathedrals praying for each other's salvation and light and breasts, until the soul illuminated its hair for a second,

who crashed through their minds in jail waiting for impossible criminals with golden heads and the charm of reality in their hearts who sang sweet blues to Alcatraz,

who retired to Mexico to cultivate a habit, or Rocky Mount to tender Buddha or Tangiers to boys or Southern Pacific to the black locomotive or Harvard to Narcissus to Woodlawn to the daisychain or grave,

who demanded sanity trials accusing the radio of hypnotism & were left with their insanity & their hands & a hung jury,

who threw potato salad at CCNY lecturers on Dadaism and subsequently presented themselves on the granite steps of the madhouse with shaven heads and harlequin speech of suicide, demanding instantaneous lobotomy,

and who were given instead the concrete void of insulin metrasol electricity hydrotherapy psychotherapy occupational therapy pingpong & amnesia,

who in humorless protest overturned only one symbolic pingpong table, resting briefly in catatonia,

returning years later truly bald except for a wig of blood, and tears and fingers, to the visible madman doom of the wards of the madtowns of the East,

Pilgrim State's Rockland's and Greystone's foetid halls, bickering with the echoes of the soul, rocking and rolling in the midnight solitude-bench dolmen-realms of love, dream of life a nightmare, bodies turned to stone as heavy as the moon,

with mother finally . . . . . , and the last fantastic book flung out of the tenement window, and the last door closed at 4 AM and the last telephone slammed at the wall in reply and the last furnished room emptied down to the last piece of mental furniture, a yellow paper rose twisted on a wire hanger in the closet, and even that imaginary, nothing but a hopeful little bit of hallucination—

ah, Carl, while you are not safe I am not safe, and now you're really in the total animal soup of time—

and who therefore ran through the icy streets obsessed with a sudden flash of the alchemy of the use of the ellipse the catalog the meter & the vibrating plane,

who dreamt and made incarnate gaps in Time & Space through images juxtaposed, and trapped the archangel of the soul between 2 visual images and joined the elemental verbs and set the noun and dash of consciousness together jumping with sensation of Pater Omnipotens Aeterna Deus

to recreate the syntax and measure of poor human prose and stand before you speechless and intelligent and shaking with shame, rejected yet confessing out the soul to conform to the rhythm of thought in his naked and endless head,

the madman bum and angel beat in Time, unknown, yet putting down here what might be left to say in time come after death,

and rose reincarnate in the ghostly clothes of jazz in the gold-horn shadow of the band and blew the suffering of America's naked mind for love into an eli eli lamma lamma sabacthani saxophone cry that shivered the cities down to the last radio

with the absolute heart of the poem of life butchered out of their own bodies good to eat a thousand years.

II

What sphinx of cement and aluminum bashed open their skulls
and ate up their brains and imagination?

Moloch! Solitude! Filth! Ugliness! Ashcans and unobtainable
dollars! Children screaming under the stairways! Boys
sobbing in armies! Old men weeping in the parks!

Moloch! Moloch! Nightmare of Moloch! Moloch the loveless!
Mental Moloch! Moloch the heavy judger of men!

Moloch the incomprehensible prison! Moloch the crossbone soul-
less jailhouse and Congress of sorrows! Moloch whose
buildings are judgment! Moloch the vast stone of war!
Moloch the stunned governments!

Moloch whose mind is pure machinery! Moloch whose blood is
running money! Moloch whose fingers are ten armies!
Moloch whose breast is a cannibal dynamo! Moloch
whose ear is a smoking tomb!

Moloch whose eyes are a thousand blind windows! Moloch
whose skyscrapers stand in the long streets like endless
Jehovahs! Moloch whose factories dream and croak in
the fog! Moloch whose smokestacks and antennae crown
the cities!

Moloch whose love is endless oil and tone! Moloch whose soul is
electricity and banks. Moloch whose poverty is the specter
of genius! Moloch whose fate is a cloud of sexless hydro-
gen! Moloch whose name is the Mind!

Moloch in whom I sit lonely! Moloch in whom I dream Angels!
Crazy in Moloch! C . . . sucker in Moloch! Lacklove and
manless in Moloch!

Moloch who entered my soul early! Moloch in whom I am a
consciousness without a body! Moloch who frightened me
out of my natural ecstasy! Moloch whom I abandon!
Wake up in Moloch! Light streaming out of the sky!

Moloch! Moloch! Robot apartments! invisible suburbs! skeleton
treasuries! blind capitals! demonic industries! spectral
nations! invincible madhouses! granite cocks! monstrous
bombs!

They broke their backs lifting Moloch to Heaven! Pavements,
  trees, radios, tons! lifting the city to Heaven which exists
  and is everywhere about us!
Visions! omens! hallucinations! miracles! ecstasies! gone down
  the American river!
Dreams! adorations! illuminations! religions the whole boatload
  of sensitive bullshit!
Breakthroughs! over the river! flips and crucifixions! gone down
  the flood! Highs! Epiphanies! Despairs! Ten years' animal
  screams and suicides! Minds! New loves! Mad generation! down on the rocks of Time!
Real holy laughter in the river! They saw it all! the wild eyes!
  the holy yells! They bade farewell! They jumped off the
  roof! to solitude! waving! carrying flowers! Down to the
  river! into the street!

III

Carl Solomon! I'm with you in Rockland
        where you're madder than I am
I'm with you in Rockland
        where you must feel very strange
I'm with you in Rockland
        where you imitate the shade of my mother
I'm with you in Rockland
        where you've murdered your twelve secretaries
I'm with you in Rockland
        where you laugh at this invisible humor
I'm with you in Rockland
        where we are great writers on the same dreadful type-
        writer
I'm with you in Rockland
        where your condition has become serious and is reported
        on the radio
I'm with you in Rockland

where the faculties of the skull no longer admit the
worms of the senses
I'm with you in Rockland
where you drink the tea of the breasts of the spinsters of
Utica
I'm with you in Rockland
where you pun on the bodies of your nurses the harpies
of the Bronx
I'm with you in Rockland
where you scream in a straightjacket that you're losing
the game of the actual pingpong of the abyss
I'm with you in Rockland
where you bang on the catatonic piano the soul is innocent and immortal it should never die ungodly in an
armed madhouse
I'm with you in Rockland
where fifty more shocks will never return your soul to
its body again from its pilgrimage to a cross in the void
I'm with you in Rockland
where you accuse your doctors of insanity and plot the
Hebrew socialist revolution against the fascist national
Golgotha
I'm with you in Rockland
where you will split the heavens of Long Island and resur-
rect your living human Jesus from the superhuman tomb
I'm with you in Rockland
where there are twenty-five thousand mad comrades all
together singing the final stanzas of the Internationale
I'm with you in Rockland
where we hug and kiss the United States under our bed-
sheets   the United States that coughs all night and won't
let us sleep
I'm with you in Rockland
where we wake up electrified out of the coma by our own
souls' airplanes roaring over the roof they've come to
drop angelic bombs the hospital illuminates itself   imaginary walls collapse   O skinny legions run outside   O

starry-spangled shocks of mercy the eternal war is here
O victory forget your underwear we're free
I'm with you in Rockland
in my dreams you walk dripping from a sea-journey on
the highway across America in tears to the door of my
cottage in the Western night

San Francisco 1955–56

FOOTNOTE TO HOWL

Holy! Holy! Holy! Holy! Holy! Holy! Holy! Holy! Holy! Holy!
Holy! Holy! Holy! Holy! Holy!
The world is holy! The soul is holy! The skin is holy! The nose is
holy! The tongue and cock and hand and asshole holy!
Everything is holy! everybody's holy! everywhere is holy! everyday is in eternity! Everyman's an angel!
The bum's as holy as the seraphim! the madman is holy as you
my soul are holy!
The typewriter is holy the poem is holy the voice is holy the
hearers are holy the ecstasy is holy!
Holy Peter holy Allen holy Solomon holy Lucien holy Kerouac
holy Huncke holy Burroughs holy Cassady holy the unknown buggered and suffering beggars holy the hideous
human angels!
Holy my mother in the insane asylum! Holy the cocks of the
grandfathers of Kansas!
Holy the groaning saxophone! Holy the bop apocalypse! Holy
the jazzbands marijuana hipsters peace & junk & drums!
Holy the solitudes of skyscrapers and pavements! Holy the
cafeterias filled with the millions! Holy the mysterious
rivers of tears under the streets!
Holy the lone juggernaut! Holy the vast lamb of the middle-
class! Holy the crazy shepherds of rebellion! Who digs
Los Angeles IS Los Angeles!
Holy New York Holy San Francisco Holy Peoria & Seattle Holy
Paris Holy Tangiers Holy Moscow Holy Istanbul!

Holy time in eternity holy eternity in time holy the clocks in
space holy the fourth dimension holy the fifth Inter-
national holy the Angel in Moloch!

Holy the sea holy the desert holy the railroad holy the locomotive holy the visions holy the hallucinations holy the
miracles holy the eyeball holy the abyss!

Holy forgiveness! mercy! charity! faith! Holy! Ours! bodies!
suffering! magnanimity!

Holy the supernatural extra brilliant intelligent kindness of the
soul!